I0082291

THE HAM FUNERAL

Patrick White

CURRENCY PRESS
performing arts publisher

CURRENCY PLAYS

First published in 1965
in *Four Plays by Patrick White*
by Eyre and Spottiswoode, London.

This edition first published in print in 1985
in *Patrick White: Collected Plays Volume I*
by Currency Press Pty Ltd,
PO Box 2287, Strawberry Hills, NSW, 2012, Australia
enquiries@currency.com.au
www.currency.com.au

Copyright © Patrick White, 1965.

Reprinted 2012, 2023

COPYING FOR EDUCATIONAL PURPOSES

The Australian *Copyright Act 1968* (Act) allows a maximum of one chapter
or 10% of this book, whichever is the greater, to be copied by any educational
institution for its educational purposes provided that that educational institution
(or the body that administers it) has given a remuneration notice to Copyright
Agency (CA) under the Act.

For details of the CA licence for educational institutions contact CA,
12/66 Goulburn Street, Sydney, NSW, 2000; tel: within Australia 1800 066 844
toll free; outside Australia +61 2 9394 7600; fax: +61 2 9394 7601; email:
memberservices@copyright.com.au

COPYING FOR OTHER PURPOSES

Except as permitted under the Act, for example a fair dealing for the purposes
of study, research, criticism or review, no part of this book may be reproduced,
stored in a retrieval system, or transmitted in any form or by any means without
prior written permission. All enquiries should be made to the publisher at the
address above.

Any performance or public reading of *The Ham Funeral* is forbidden unless
a licence has been received from the author's estate or the author's agent. The
purchase of this book in no way gives the purchaser the right to perform the play
in public, whether by means of a staged production or a reading. All applications
for public performance should be addressed to Jane Novak, PO Box 894,
Broadway NSW 2007; email: jane@janenovak.com

NATIONAL LIBRARY OF AUSTRALIA CIP DATA

Author:	White, Patrick, 1912–1990.
Title:	The ham funeral / Patrick White.
ISBN:	9780868199627 (pbk.)
Subjects:	Australian drama–20th century.
Dewey Number:	A822.3

Typeset by Dean Nottle for Currency Press.
Cover design by Lisa White for Currency Press.

Currency Press acknowledges the Traditional Owners of the Country on which
we live and work. We pay our respects to all Aboriginal and Torres Strait
Islander Elders, past and present.

Contents

The Ham Funeral was first performed by the Adelaide University Guild at the Union Theatre, Adelaide, on 15 November 1961 with the following cast:

YOUNG MAN	John Adams
LANDLADY	Joan Bruce
LANDLORD	Hedley Cullen
GIRL	Anne Dibden
FIRST LADY	Pat Griffith
SECOND LADY	Kathleen Steele-Scott
FIRST RELATIVE	Dennis Olsen
SECOND RELATIVE	Don Porter
THIRD RELATIVE	Tony Georgeson
FOURTH RELATIVE	Brian Bergin

Directed by John Tasker
Designed by S. Ostoja Kotkowski

CHARACTERS

LANDLORD
LANDLADY
YOUNG MAN
GIRL
TWO LADIES
FOUR RELATIVES

SETTING

A lodging house and the streets of London, about 1919.

ACT ONE

Before the curtain rises, the YOUNG MAN *appears, and speaks the following prologue. He is dressed informally, in a fashion which could be about 1919. He is rather pale. His attitude throughout the play is a mixture of the intent and the absent, aggressiveness and diffidence.*

YOUNG MAN: [*yawning, addressing the audience*] I have just woken, it seems. It is about... well, the time doesn't matter. The same applies to my origins. It could be that I was born in Birmingham... or Brooklyn... or Murwillumbah. What is important is that, thanks to a succession of meat pies (the gristle-and-gravy, cardboard kind) and many cups of pink tea, I am alive! Therefore... and this is the rather painful point... I must go in soon and take part in the play, which, as usual, is a piece about eels. As I am also a poet... though, to be perfectly honest, I have not yet found out for sure... my dilemma in the play is how to take part in the conflict of eels, and survive at the same time... becoming a kind of Roman candle... fizzing forever in the dark. [*Somewhat stern*] Probably quite a number of you are wondering by now whether this is your kind of play. I'm sorry to have to announce the management won't refund any money. You must simply sit it out, and see whether you can't recognise some of the forms that will squirm before you in this mad, muddy mess of eels. As it heaves and shudders, you may even find... you have begun to feed... on memory... [*More relaxed, as if returning to his private world*] Let me remind you of a great, damp, crumbling house in which people are living. Remember? Perhaps you have only dreamt it. Some of the doors of the house have never been seen open. The people whose protection they are intended to ensure can be heard bumping about behind them. Sometimes these characters fry little meals for their temporary comfort. Sometimes it sounds as though they are breaking glass. As far as we know, nobody has ever committed a murder in this house of ours, but it could be... [*Slowing up, thoughtfully*] Certainly murder has often been contemplated... [*looking at his wristwatch*] ... towards five o'clock... when the fingers have turned to bones... and the sky is green. There are the voices, too. Not only the voices of the walls. There are the voices of the gas fires, full of advice that we haven't the courage to take. And the mirrors in the deal dressing tables... well, you can never believe them. They are living lies, down to the last vein in their eyeballs. So, we turn our backs. But look again. The landlady, you're going to see, spends an awful lot of her time looking again. And I... but I know already. I know too much. That is the poet's tragedy. To know too much, and never enough. [*Defensive*] You are right in suspecting I can't give you a message. The message always gets torn up. It lies at the bottom of the basket, under the hair, and everything else. Don't suggest we piece it together. I've found the answer is always different. So... the most I can do is give you the play, and plays, of course, are only plays. Even the great play of life. Some of you will argue that that is real enough... [*very quiet and diffident*] ... but can we be... sure? [*Returning to the surface, dry*] Thank you. We'd better begin now.

He exits behind the curtain.

SCENE ONE

The curtain rises on Scene One. The basement of the lodging house— that is, the lower half of the picture; for the present the stairwell, back, and the hall and two ground floor bedrooms, above, remain in darkness. Back centre is a door standing open on the darkened stairwell. Right and left are the area windows, through which the light palely filters. Against the wall, right, is an enormous iron bedstead with brass knobs. A kitchen table, centre. At least six kitchen chairs, some at the table, some dispersed. Against the wall, left, a gas stove of an antique variety, and a dresser. The action of the play will also reveal that there is an invisible dressing table against the 'fourth wall', so that anybody making use of the mirror must expose themselves fully to the audience. An invisible sink against the same 'wall', to the left, on the kitchen half of the basement. The whole is lit by an isolated, unshaded electric bulb.

The LANDLORD *is seated on one of the deal chairs beside the kitchen table. He sits with his legs apart, facing the audience. He is a vast man, swollen, dressed from neck to ankle in woollen underclothes, of a greyish colour, and in carpet slippers. His face is pallid, flushing to strawberry in the nose, and with a wen on one cheek. He wears a thick, drooping moustache, and is smoking a short, black pipe. The* LANDLADY *is also seated at the kitchen table, with a saucepan, peeling potatoes. She is a large woman in the dangerous forties, ripe and bursting. Her hair, still black, is swept up untidily in a vaguely Edwardian coiffure. She is wearing a shabby, white satin blouse, dark skirt, and an old pair of pink mules. She continues to peel potatoes, but with mounting boredom and distaste.*

LANDLADY: [*laying down the knife, pushing things away from her*] I'm just about sick of peelin' bloody pertaters! Don't yer understand, Will? [*Disgusted*] You wouldn't!

> LANDLORD *looks at her expressionlessly for a moment, then continues to stare and smoke.*

I'm sick of it! I'm sick…

LANDLORD: Why?

LANDLADY: Why? Lord, I dunno why! [*She yawns and stretches.*] Aooh, nao! [*Then relaxes on her chair, momentarily helpless.*] I dunno much. Else I wouldn't be sitting 'ere. Thursday I went to the theayter. It was lovely. A bunch of toffs in satin… gassin' about love and nothink. An' when I come out, the rain 'ad stopped, an' the blossom sticky on the chestnut trees. You could smell it, that strong and funny. It nearly bust my 'ead open… [*Angrily, pushing the potato peelings farther away from her*] Then I come 'ome!

> LANDLORD *noisily clears his throat.*

Yes, that's wot I felt! Twenty years listenin' to the damp, an' the furniture, an' your 'usband's breathin'!

> LANDLADY *gets up, goes to the invisible dressing table in the 'fourth wall', looking into the mirror, touching her hair.*

[*Sighing*] Twenty years, an' more, since that day at 'Ighgate… [*Seductively, more to the mirror than to her husband*] Remember? I said: 'P'raps the grass ain't quite dry'. ''Oo cares,' says you. I says: 'Not me'. I was a bit afraid. 'Ow your breath scorched, Will. I seen the pores of yer skin, like they was in one of them mikerscopes. You smelled of soap an' beer. I could feel me own breath, strugglin' to fan your fire. Well, we was burnt. We was burnt up. Now I listen to you breathe, and it's regular as the silence and the clocks.

LANDLORD *heaves a snorting sigh, but whether in sympathy or contempt, it is not possible to tell.*

[*Pulling herself together*] But I got used to it. The way you do get used to things. The way the iron becomes part of the tree, when it's eaten into it...

She goes and puts her hand on his shoulder, so that for the moment they make a monumental, if primitive whole.

I loved you, Will. Afterwards, I even got to like yer, and wanted you about. We were two bodies in the bed. I could return to you out of my dreams... push against your hot side. You didn't wake, ever. But you was solid.

LANDLORD *grunts and stares.*

[*Withdrawing her hand, angrily*] You were that, alright!

She carries potato peelings and disposes of them briskly, somewhere near the stove, left.

Anyway, 'ere's for a cup of tea. And a slice of somethink. I'm 'ungry.

She takes down a teapot from the dresser.

LANDLORD: You're always 'ungry.

LANDLADY: [*laughing, good-natured now, as she goes to the kettle to warm the pot*] Yes. I am. [*Coming forward to the invisible sink, to swill and empty the pot*] I like to eat. I like somethink you can get yer tongue round. A nice piece of fat 'am, for instance. [*Emptying the pot into the sink*] Or a little bowl of stewed eels. Or a chop with the kidney on it. Or even a bit of bread and drippin', with the brown underneath. [*Filling the pot with tea at the dresser*] Yes, there's no end to pleasure, if yer come to think. [*Having filled the pot with hot water, she stands it on the table. Thoughtfully*] That reminds me, Will...

LANDLORD *stares and smokes.*

... that young man upstairs... beats me wot pleasure 'e gets. 'E don't go nowhere. Lies an' sleeps, or stares at the ceilin', as if 'e was sick... or barmy.

LANDLORD: [*grunting*] 'E's a poet.

LANDLADY: 'E's a bloomin' corpse for all the life 'e lives. Lyin' with 'is 'ands under 'is 'ead. An', d'you know, Will, once I caught 'im listenin' at the room opposite. Settled down to it, proper, like. [*She starts to bring cups.*] You would'uv said 'is ear was growin' out of the door.

LANDLORD: Up to no good.

LANDLADY: [*giggling*] Wot! D'you mean Phyllis Pither? Oh, my!

LANDLORD: Ain't she t'other side of the door?

LANDLADY: Yes.

LANDLORD: Well.

LANDLADY: Go on! Phyllis Pither! [*She starts to cut slices of bread.*] Nao, serious, Will. I feel sorry for that young man. Let's ask 'im down now and again, and act a bit sociable. [*Withdrawing into herself for a moment*] Jack would'uv been 'is age by now. [*Coaxingly*] Eh? Feed 'im up a bit. The skin under 'is eyes 'as turned quite blue. Wot do you say, Will?

LANDLORD *grunts.*

That's right. Knew you'd come round. You're not a bad stick. [*She wipes her hands on a towel.*] Does you good to 'ave company once in a while. [*She goes quickly to the dressing table mirror in the 'fourth wall', and touches her hair.*] A fresh face, an' you forget yer own. [*Meditatively*] When I walk down the street, I often feel I could take the faces... I could eat 'em up. If they only knew! But there they are... [*disgusted*] ... they might be a lot of cherry stones! [*She touches her own face and frowns.*] Makes yer sick! [*She turns quickly.*] Well, I'll fetch 'im down... [*Pausing as she catches sight of* LANDLORD'*s figure*] I say, Will, wot about you in them old underwears?

LANDLORD: [*staring in front of him, without flinching*] Wot's wrong?

LANDLADY: Why, nothink... I suppose...

She goes out, back. As she does so, the basement darkens, and the stairway, and hall above, centre, are illuminated.

SCENE TWO

The stairs.

LANDLADY: [*pausing at the stairs*] This part of the 'ouse 'as never been warmed. I bet not even a first-class weddin' could chafe life into the stairs. Not all the rice an' rudery in the world. [*Starting to mount*] I've always been a bit afraid... A lady could get 'er neck broke... not by fallin', neither. [*Mounting*] The mice squeak behind the skirtin' boards. Look 'ow the damp's spread. You could teach geography off of the wall. [*Pausing as she mounts, tracing an outline with her finger*] 'Ole continents to them that knows. Africa couldn't be darker to me. Once I almost screamed. Then I wondered if anyone would 'ear me. Other people are deaf, you know. [*Getting her breath*] I hate the stairs. There's a great deal I hate. There's a lot that refuses to be loved. [*Reaching the hall above*] I could love, too, if they'd let me. [*Pausing for a moment by the street door*] Once I heard a voice in the street, somebody trying to get in. But when I opened, 'e said it was the wrong door.

> *She approaches the door of young man's bedroom. This occupies the upper left part of the stage.*

[*Pausing outside, listening*] Listen! You can 'ear 'im. You can 'ear 'im already. Lyin' on the bed. Doin' nothink. Once 'e wrote a poem. I picked it out of the basket, along with the razor blades, and a piece of lilac 'e must 'ave pinched from somewhere. I couldn't read 'is poem, but the paper was still warm, as if 'e'd clenched it quite a while. Although 'e's been 'ere all these months... or is it years?... I'm buggered if I can remember 'is name. I call 'im Jack. [*She knocks on the door.*] Hey, are you there, young man? 'S me, Jack. Can you 'ear? Or am I speakin' to a dummy?

SCENE THREE

Young man's bedroom.

In the silence following the LANDLADY*'s words, the room floods with a pale afternoon light. There is a window, back, a black branch with a few early leaves cutting across the pane. A narrow iron bed with head against the wall, left. A crimson plush armchair, with comfortable, rounded shoulders, right forward. Against the 'fourth wall' there would be a dressing table. The young man's coat is hanging from a hook on the door leading to the hall.*

The YOUNG MAN *himself is stretched on the bed, in shirt and trousers, and wearing his shoes. His hands are behind his head, and he is staring at the ceiling.*

YOUNG MAN: [*to* LANDLADY, *as she waits for admission*] It's your house, and the door isn't locked.

He continues to stare at the ceiling.

LANDLADY: [*opening the door, entering*] That's a nice thing to say to a lady 'oo means well. Not up yet, eh? [*She wanders about the room, touching things.*] And 'ere it is... evenin'. A nice evenin', too. A bit raw, but 'ealthy like. [*Looking out of the window*] There's the girls goin' on the job. Their 'ips 'aven't loosened yet. They've still got to warm the pavement. [*Turning back into the room*] An' you not up! Well, I suppose you're yer own master.

YOUNG MAN: [*wryly, still staring at the ceiling*] I like to think so.

LANDLADY: A poet, anyways.

YOUNG MAN: Once I wrote a poem...

LANDLADY: That was the one I found in the basket.

YOUNG MAN *immediately raises himself on an elbow. Looks at her.*

Not that I read it, of course. I never could read an educated 'and.

YOUNG MAN *sinks back on the bed, apparently satisfied.*

But I like a good bit of poetry. I love a love poem. [*Sighing*] Yes.

YOUNG MAN: [*again rising on his elbow, looking at her*] Tell me, Mrs Lusty, do you expect much of life?

LANDLADY: Expect? I don't expect. I take wot turns up.

YOUNG MAN: I hope I still expect.

LANDLADY: [*yawning*] You're barmy. Or clever.

She sits down comfortably in the plush chair.

YOUNG MAN: [*propped on his elbow, looking inward at his own experience*] I'm certainly not clever. Sometimes my lack of cleverness makes me desperate. It seems that everybody else understands which button to press, which lever to pull, which tablet to take, to achieve the maximum happiness or the required dream. At least, that's what their faces claim. Sometimes I stand in the street and watch them. Then my ignorance begins to choke me. The answer is either tremendously simple, or tremendously involved. But either way, it's something I still fail to grasp.

LANDLADY: You poor kid!

YOUNG MAN: When I was a boy, I mooned about in a garden. I tried to fit words to the sounds of nature and the shape of lilacs.

LANDLADY: Always said you was a screw loose!

YOUNG MAN: No-one before myself had ever heard or seen. I had to prove it. Then I found I couldn't. [*He slips back to his original position, staring at the ceiling.*] Or I haven't yet.

LANDLADY: Don't lose 'eart. You'll write lots of lovely poems.

YOUNG MAN: [*laughing*] Since they fetched up their breakfast, men are less inclined to listen to the cuckoo. And I'm not reconciled to the stench of vomit.

LANDLADY: Eh?

YOUNG MAN: Nothing. [*Turning on his side to look at her*] How you long to be kind. You'd like to devour the world, and keep it warm inside you. But as that isn't possible, you touch, and touch, and touch, and offer slices of bread smeared with rancid dripping.

LANDLADY: Wot if I was goin' ter suggest you come and 'ave a bite with me and my old man! There's no 'arm done. There's nothing like food in yer stummick for putting things right in yer head. [*Advancing on him, taking his hand*] And if I take your hand, it's because it's cold, Jack. It is. Cold as a dead canary's claw.

YOUNG MAN: [*withdrawing his hand quickly, looking at it*] My name is not Jack.

LANDLADY: It might have been.

YOUNG MAN: [*making to ward her off with his elbow*] Are you going to touch me again?

LANDLADY: Death itself couldn't touch you, yer little bastard!

YOUNG MAN: Oh, dear Mrs Lusty, I'm all you say. But admitting doesn't help. Now tell me about your poor dead child.

LANDLADY: There's nothink to tell. There wasn't time. 'E died. It was Saint Swithin's Day. That's all.

YOUNG MAN: Sad. But it might have been sadder. He might have sprouted from your area, all muscles and malignancy, and overrun the world. Or they might have stoned him for a saint. Or he could have turned out so pale, nobody noticed him.

LANDLADY: Whichever way, 'e would 'uv needed 'is tea.

YOUNG MAN: [*sitting up, dangling his legs over the side of the bed*] How remorseless you are! And I my bread and dripping.

LANDLADY: You'll come then, Jack? It'll liven Will up.

YOUNG MAN: [*grimacing*] He's landlord enough dead. Can't imagine him alive.

LANDLADY: Will's alright.

YOUNG MAN: Everything's 'alright'. The pity is it's never 'better'.

LANDLADY: [*limping and wincing as she goes towards the door*] Tonight my bunion 'urts like 'ell. Wonder wot that means?

YOUNG MAN: An accident. Or just a letter… the most brutal of all threats… Or perhaps a stranger opening the door… her arms full of flowers…

LANDLADY: We don't get no strangers 'ere.

YOUNG MAN: [*cautiously*] Tell me, Mrs Lusty, before you go, what is in the room across the hall?

LANDLADY: Why, it's me other front room.

YOUNG MAN: Just another bedroom.

LANDLADY: In every way h'identical.

YOUNG MAN: And occupied…

LANDLADY: Since I don't know when.

YOUNG MAN: Sometimes she puts her mouth to the door. I can almost hear the words if I hold my ear…

LANDLADY: She wouldn't be so bold!

YOUNG MAN: I can hear her skirt rubbing the paper. It has the sound of very thin ice. The air is filled with intolerable lilacs…

LANDLADY: Potty, that's wot you are! I always said. There's no-one but Phyllis Pither in there. A young lady as works for a firm of gasfitters in Kennington. In every way a steady girl. Gives 'er wages to an auntie 'oo suffers from Bright's Disease…

YOUNG MAN: … filling the air, heavier than eyelids…

LANDLADY: … Phyllis leaves early, an' comes 'ome late. Most nights she goes to bed with an aspirin and a cold.

YOUNG MAN: [*jumping off the bed*] I am exorcised! Or am I?

LANDLADY: Aoh, come on! Stop yer jaw! [*She moves towards the door.*] My tongue's 'angin' out for a cuppa.

> LANDLADY *goes into the hall.*

YOUNG MAN: Yes. I'm coming.

LANDLADY: A proper windbag!

> *Exit* LANDLADY *down the dark stairs.*

> [*Still grumbling*] My feet ache that bad… I could'uv walked all the way from Putney…

> *She goes into the still unlit kitchen.*

YOUNG MAN *makes sure she has gone. Leaves his room, crosses the hall to the door of the second bedroom, left. Leans against the door, arms outstretched, cheek pressed to the panel.*

YOUNG MAN: All my life the present moment has just failed to materialise. Completeness is something I sense, but never yet experienced. There is always the separating wall.

On the other side of the door a patch of light forms, in which are visible a hand and an arm in a long white glove. The fingers barely rest on the intervening door, at the point where the YOUNG MAN'*s head is resting on the other side. The hand remains motionless, but with a kind of still grace and poetry.*

Often I hear your voice. But the words remain indistinct. I could swear to the touch of your fingers, without actual pressure. If I could feel certain, this door might vanish. Or am I just an impostor... trying to draw a bouquet out of the air, without having learnt the trick? Or is there? Or is there a bouquet? Where are the stiff flowers, trembling on their wire stems?

LANDLADY: [*calling impatiently from the kitchen below*] Hey, Jack, wotcher playin' at? I like ter know 'ow I stand. Are yer comin', or aren't yer? 'Ere's this nice tea, stewin' in the pot...

YOUNG MAN: Is this the most we can expect? The figures in the basement? The silent landlord and his bursting wife...

Light in the second bedroom fades. YOUNG MAN *winces against the separating door.*

[*Striking the door with palm of his hand*] I've had my answer! I hold my still, cold poem, stiller and colder than the landlady's dead child... [*He tears himself away from the door with an effort. Calling to* LANDLADY] Coming, Mrs Lusty!

He dashes into his room, snatches the coat from the hook behind the door. As the lower stairs light up, he is back in the hall. The bedroom fades.

[*Running downstairs, bundling into his coat, calling*] Don't say I ever spoilt a party! I'll be there before my own voice!

SCENE FOUR

The basement floods with light and the stairs fade as YOUNG MAN *enters.* LANDLORD *is sitting in exactly the same position as before.* LANDLADY *is back at the kitchen table, cutting slices of bread, and spreading them with dripping.*

YOUNG MAN: [*entering, to* LANDLORD] How're they treatin' yer, Mr Lusty?

> *He sleeks down his hair. His manner has become cocky, and rather vulgar.* LANDLORD *does not answer. Sits staring ahead, smoking.*

[*Rubbing his hands together, heartily*] I'm fine meself. Thanks for inquiring. [*Panting*] On these fresh spring evenings my breff goes on ahead like the spirit of health.

LANDLADY: [*on her dignity, spreading dripping*] I thought you'd died.

> *A silence.*

YOUNG MAN: [*himself again*] I might have. Or someone. To justify this funeral.

LANDLADY: 'Ere, young man! Elders and betters, you know. An' drippin' thrown in. Let us talk about somethink nice and bright. There's other flowers besides everlastin's. [*Pushing tea and bread and dripping towards* YOUNG MAN] An' you, Will Lusty… [*passing same to her husband*] tell us a story of yer youth, when you threw the big buck nigger on the grass, and I kissed you on the mouth 'cause I was proud.

LANDLORD: [*spitting out a mouthful, throwing the slice back on the plate*] This stinks! It stinks!

YOUNG MAN: It might, too.

LANDLADY: It's you, Will. Your bloody mouth's foul with silence.

YOUNG MAN: [*mock heroic*] Then she threw 'im on the grass, 'is muscles turned to fat!

> LANDLORD *calmly wipes the stem of his pipe on his arm, re-lights, and continues smoking.*

LANDLADY: [*to* YOUNG MAN] No-one asked lip from you.

YOUNG MAN: That was irony, Mrs Lusty. I'd no more think of offering you cheek than I'd throw a pat of butter to a steamroller.

LANDLADY: [*tearfully*] All you get is words... good, bad, or doubtful. Or else it's silence. [*She shivers.*] That's worse.

LANDLORD: Yes, you suffer, Alma Lusty!

LANDLADY: Wot come over you? I wasn't askin' for sympathy.

LANDLORD: You ask me for the story of me youth. You'd ask me in the same breath for a basinful of blood.

YOUNG MAN: [*rubbing his hands*] Ding dong! Now they're at it!

LANDLADY: [*raucously contemptuous*] This is Christmas! Will Lusty found 'is tongue! If a court'ud asked me was you still there, I wouldn't 'uv known wot to answer. Reminds me of a kid I used to be friendly with... got me to take a squint at a fart 'e'd caught in a bottle...

LANDLORD: Well?

LANDLADY: ''Oo's to know,' I says, 'if it didn't get away?'

LANDLORD: And wot did 'e say to that?

LANDLADY: [*tossing her head, out of patience*] Aoh, I forget!

LANDLORD: Never knowed Alma to forget.

LANDLADY: [*emphasising with one fingertip on the table*] The point is, Will, you've e-vap-er-ated! [*She smiles to herself, smugly pleased.*] See? You went an' left us.

LANDLORD: If I left yer, something must'uv brought me back.

LANDLADY *hunches her shoulders, grits her teeth.*

LANDLADY: All your life you wasn't there! All your life!

LANDLORD: 'Arp! 'Arp! My life's been that simple, it doesn't bear tellin' about. I was a boy. I grew. I met a woman 'oo became my wife...

LANDLADY: That was simple! Lord save us!

LANDLORD: We bought the little sweet shop out at Croakers' Pond...

LANDLADY: [*sentimental*] The little sweet shop!

LANDLORD: ... because you thought you fancied it. Well, we sold the little business. You said the bell made yer nervous. I took up wrestlin'... for the exercise. Then I found I could do it good.

LANDLADY: You did it good...

LANDLORD: [*moved and repelled*] I can't add nothink to that. It's done. I threw Joe 'Arris, and Billy Doyle, and Patsy Lonergan. I 'eld 'em to the ground till their ribs and thighs was crackin'. I could feel the whole world give in me hands. The mob would let fly with their caps and their voices. An' there was always one tart louder than the rest.

She told me I'd won. She told me I was Gawd. Then, when I could
no longer 'old their faces in the dust, an' the stink of sweat 'ad begun
to make me sicken, she let me know we'd reached 'ell by a short cut.

LANDLADY: It's 'arder for the woman. The woman's the man's shadow.

LANDLORD: Listen to the tap drip in the sink. Listen to its words. Soft
and pitiful. We promise ourselves we'll change the washer. But we
don't.

YOUNG MAN: Is this a tragedy? Or is it two fat people in a basement,
turning on each other?

LANDLADY: But it's life I'm after, Will. [*With a vague gesture*] That's
why I can't stick all this. That's why the old days are still glossy as
a postcard.

LANDLORD: [*shifting his thighs, contemptuously*] Life!

LANDLADY: I can taste the whelks! I can hear the flares! You can see
right inside of a person by the light of acetylene flares.

LANDLORD: I sit 'ere. I am content. Life, at last, is wherever a man
'appens to be. This 'ouse is life. I watch it fill with light, an' darken.
These are my days and nights. The solid 'ouse spreadin' above my
head. Only once in a while I remember the naked bodies... knotting
together... killing theirselves... and one another... Bloody deluded!

YOUNG MAN: He's a sensitive beast, this landlord, inside his underclothes.
And I disliked him. I loathed him. I was almost afraid. Perhaps this
is why.

LANDLADY: But it's natural, Will, to fight. And love.

LANDLORD: [*laughing in his throat, speaking not particularly to his wife,
spreading his hand on the tabletop*] This table is love... if you can get
to know it...

LANDLADY: [*going and leaning on the dresser, left, her hands in her
thick hair, in an attitude of desperation and boredom, choking*] I'll
suffocate!

YOUNG MAN: And my lungs are bursting, with enthusiasm and excitement... now that his flesh has opened, and I look inside. [*Moving his
chair closer to* LANDLORD] Perhaps he can answer questions. I no
longer notice the knob on his face.

   LANDLADY *turns suddenly.*

LANDLADY: [*menacing*] You keep off!

YOUNG MAN: [*turning to her, in amazement*] I had forgotten the landlady.

LANDLORD *sits as before, intent on some problem of his own.*

LANDLADY: Everyone forgets the landlady. [*To* YOUNG MAN] But you ought to remember.

YOUNG MAN: I? I don't understand.

LANDLADY: [*laughing*] Oh, they're all alike! 'Cold puddin' is cold puddin',' they say, 'It didn't oughta be warmed up.' [*Half angry, half tender*] But warmth... warmth is everything. [*Advancing on* YOUNG MAN] Pretendin' to forget!

YOUNG MAN: [*cocking an eye at* LANDLORD, *speaking with the same vulgar assurance he assumed on his entrance*] What price the landlord now? You win, Alma! You always did!

LANDLADY: [*putting her arms around his neck, at the same time standing back so as to look at him, laughing sensually and relieved*] I knew you'd remember. You can remember each line we wrote to the poste restante. You can remember the leg above the boot. They was a pretty little pair of boots. Glassy kid. I can remember the taste of seaweed on your mouth. Up on the promenade, the band had started on 'The Quaker Girl'. As if you could forget! Why, Fred!

YOUNG MAN: [*not quite freed from his own identity*] Fred?

LANDLORD *slams his hand on the table, and quivers.*

LANDLADY: [*looking at* LANDLORD, *shouting vindictively*] Wot if I said it!

She pushes aside YOUNG MAN, *who has only been instrumental in evoking the scene.*

LANDLORD: You bitch! I told you to never...

LANDLADY: As if it wasn't finished! But 'ow can I forget wot I can still feel?

LANDLORD: You bitch!

YOUNG MAN: [*to himself*] Am I the chorus to this play? No-one ever cursed the chorus. Serpents only slither from the sea to strangle those who are big enough.

LANDLORD: [*contemptuously, to* LANDLADY] Because you can still feel! [*He wipes his face with his hand. Speaking with great emotion, although restrained*] Only once I set eyes on Him... before 'e disappeared... in the rain, an' the gaslight... Did I say only once?

YOUNG MAN: [*still a chorus to the drama*] You did, Landlord. But the room still quivers.

A brief silence.

LANDLORD: [*producing a recollection from the depths*] Well, I seen 'im again… in the face of that dead kid. I seen that little blue, queasy, wizened pimp… lookin' at me out of the coffin… through the closed eyelids. You'd pulled a piece of geranium, an' stuck it in 'is… you couldn't 'ardly call it a hand. I never smelt geranium since without I felt choked.

LANDLADY: [*holding herself, in agony*] Wot of it? I 'ad a child. For a few days I held 'im in my arms. 'Oose child? 'Oo cares!

YOUNG MAN: I could offer pity. But pity is an abstraction of other people's sorrows.

LANDLORD: [*to* LANDLADY] You admit alright…

LANDLADY: I 'ad a child. It died. That's all I admit.

LANDLORD: The little, blue-faced, wizened pimp!

LANDLADY: [*bowing her head*] I admit that 'urts still.

YOUNG MAN: Now, where's the landlord, whose words for a moment brought the furniture to life? He's about to eat his wisdom. He's still only a man!

LANDLORD *has raised himself heavily but methodically out of his chair. Staggers towards* LANDLADY.

LANDLORD: [*hitting her over the side of the face*] The little bastard!

A silence before LANDLADY *speaks.*

LANDLADY: I can't cry, Will. I loved 'im…

LANDLORD *returns heavily to his chair, sits in the same position as before.*

YOUNG MAN: [*moved*] In the end, there is nothing I can do to cut their tangle. They must fumble, and bungle, and loosen the knot for themselves.

YOUNG MAN *turns towards the stairs, back.*

LANDLADY: [*to* LANDLORD] … just as I loved you, Will. And other men. Or tried to. Only it dies too soon. It dies in your arms.

The basement darkens.

SCENE FIVE

The stairs.

The stairs come to life as YOUNG MAN *mounts with apparent weariness and disillusion.*

YOUNG MAN: [*sighing, counting to himself*] One... two... three... In the evening a mute monotony fills the stairs... the resentment of all the feet that ever trod the carpet. Look. The cockroach popped by the landlady's old pink slipper... There's the corner where a friend, or lover, was overcome by Saturday night... and the stair where the broken rod was never replaced... not even after the plumber took a tumble... Fatal, melancholy, passionate moments crowd upon the stairs... but none of them ever broke the monotony for long... So resentment creeps back... and back... as we mount... endlessly...

Emerging at the top, he comes forward, facing the audience.

[*Somewhat breathless after negotiating the stairs*] ... hoping to burst out... show we are independent creatures... no connection with the landlord and his wife... only waiting to be recognised... for our brilliant minds, noble instincts, romantic appearance, generous acts! [*Pause.*] Strange we have been overlooked... It can't continue. It won't! [*Pause.*] But the silent house doesn't confirm. It only echoes. [*Turning, going towards his room*] The evenings of spring are merciless.

He goes into his room, which lightens as the stairs fade.

Purpose dwindles... if one ever had a purpose... [*Almost in a panic*] What... what is intended? [*Desperate*] If one could only... find... out...

He goes back quickly and purposefully into the hall.

[*Approaching the door of the bedroom opposite*] If you would tell me! You!

Light drifts through the second bedroom, which occupies the upper right-hand portion of the stage. It is, as the landlady said, furnished in exactly the same way as the room occupied by the YOUNG MAN—*iron bed, plush chair, etc., disposed as already described. Centre, facing the closed door which* YOUNG MAN *is addressing, a* GIRL *is seated—upright, grave, dressed very simply and unobtrusively, in white. Her fair hair is worn long. Her expression is remote, but radiant.*

GIRL: Yes?

YOUNG MAN: [*smiling, incredulously*] Ah, you are there then! Door or no door, I can tell when it happens. [*He goes and stands close to the door, cheek against it, eyes closed, smiling and content.*] You are very close now. But I hoped you would tell me how I might come closer.

GIRL: [*gently, but firmly*] That is something which can't be taught.

YOUNG MAN: I was afraid of that.

GIRL: You're afraid of so much.

YOUNG MAN: Who isn't?

GIRL: I am not.

YOUNG MAN: There! You become remote again.

GIRL: Shall I show you how close? As a little boy you would gobble angelica and cherries, and afterwards look for somebody to blame.

YOUNG MAN: Intuition itself! Tell me some more.

GIRL *leaves the chair, comes to the separating door standing close to it, so that she is in more or less the same position as* YOUNG MAN *on the other side.*

GIRL: Alright. What would you like to hear?

YOUNG MAN: Usually I don't have to tell you.

GIRL: [*her voice intimate, but distinct*] The mountain? The mist was cold behind your bare knees. The valleys were rolling with the white mist. The parrots flew screaming... the wedge of black cockatoos... You held the sheet of paper in your hand. You had not yet found words...

YOUNG MAN: Yes? But now your voice sounds distant.

GIRL: Distant as childhood.

YOUNG MAN: [*impatient*] Yes, yes! Go on!

GIRL: Where the shrubbery ended, there was an oval bed of lilacs, which remained wet even after the sun had risen above the cypresses. The long, bosomy sprays of lilac would press against your soaking shirt... the dreamy scents drench you with words and longing. The sun was rising... rising... bursting on the crests of the trees. You were on the verge! Then, suddenly, you had never felt emptier... and went away sneezing... and didn't stop all that spring. So they sent you to live in a climate where the landscape had been drained of every possible excitement and interest... dry... healthy... interminable.

YOUNG MAN: That was a bit of an anti-climax!

GIRL: So was adolescence.

YOUNG MAN: Where do we go from there?

Pause.

GIRL: I should really leave you. Unless...

YOUNG MAN: [*desperate*] You're going to deny me the little you give?

GIRL: [*yawning*] The question is: What do you make of it? The answer: Nothing.

YOUNG MAN: [*downcast*] I agree. I haven't yet. But if you remain the other side of the door, we can never complete each other.

GIRL: [*sharply, raising her head*] Complete!

YOUNG MAN: A comfortable, smug, even ugly word... but desirable.

GIRL: [*sternly*] For you, death in two syllables.

YOUNG MAN: [*beating on the door with his hands*] Then tell me what is the most I can expect? How am I to discover?

GIRL: [*stalling*] Discover?

She retreats to the centre of her room and, at the same time, YOUNG MAN *seems propelled like an automaton, back from the door, across the hall, to the centre of his.*

It is in the air, it is in the wall...

She goes back, feverishly, stands looking out of her window. Simultaneously, YOUNG MAN *goes to his.*

... the bough taps out the answer on the window. It is even in the basement... where the landlord's teeth have left their bite in the stale crust, and potato peelings are oracles to those who learn how to read them.

She has moved restlessly back to her position at the door, but YOUNG MAN, *while beginning to follow suit, firmly resists the impulse on mention of the basement, and remains standing centre of his own room.*

YOUNG MAN: You, too, point to the basement! I hadn't bargained for that.

GIRL: We're inclined to overlook the landlord.

YOUNG MAN: [*as if asleep*] The landlord said… What was it the landlord said?

GIRL: [*moving restlessly back to the centre of her room*] Ah, what was it?

YOUNG MAN: [*driven, sleepwalking*] I must ask… [*Moving towards the door which connects with the hall*] I must ask the landlord.

GIRL: Too late…

Girl's bedroom fades, as a scream is heard from the dark of the basement. It is the LANDLADY'*s voice.* YOUNG MAN *stands transfixed, listening, centre of his room.*

YOUNG MAN: [*whispering*] Too late…

He goes quickly into the hall, to the door of the second bedroom.

[*Calling*] You, there! [*Shouting*] When I need your advice most, you leave me!

LANDLADY *is heard crying and lamenting in the dark.*

LANDLADY'S VOICE: Ah, Will, Will, you haven't left me!

YOUNG MAN: [*to himself, facing the audience*] Which of us is more lost, the landlady or I, it is difficult to say.

LANDLADY'S VOICE: [*calling from the dark, apparently to* YOUNG MAN] Where are yer? Where are yer? Am I alone in this great damp house?

YOUNG MAN: [*righting his collar, calling*] Coming, Mrs Lusty!

As he races down the stairs they light up. The hall and stairs fade as soon as he enters the basement.

SCENE SIX

The basement.

The basement lights up as YOUNG MAN *reaches the bottom of the stairs. Same as before, except that* LANDLORD *is now lying on the floor beside his chair, his pipe dropped somewhere near him.* LANDLADY *is kneeling, bending over him, trying to warm, envelop him.*

LANDLADY: [*blubbering*] Dear Will! Speak! Just one word, Will. It's me. I know! I know! But speak!

As YOUNG MAN *enters, he hesitates a moment in the doorway.*
[*On her knees, turning to address him*] See, boy... Will... died.

YOUNG MAN: [*preparing to protest*] But he can't...

LANDLADY: [*laying her open hand on* LANDLORD's *eyes, wiping his face with her apron*] He's gone. I know. The life'd left 'im already before I touched 'im. Will is dead!

YOUNG MAN: [*coming forward slowly*] Have it your own way then.

LANDLADY: [*looking down*] That's wot Will used to say. Well, 'e's said it for the last time.

YOUNG MAN: [*absorbed by the sight of the dead* LANDLORD] Who would really believe there could ever be a last time?

YOUNG MAN *continues staring closely at* LANDLORD.

LANDLADY: Wot are yer starin' at?

YOUNG MAN: I've never seen a dead body...

LANDLADY: [*as the truth sweeps over her afresh*] Will... a dead...

She cannot restrain herself.

YOUNG MAN: [*shaking her*] Mrs Lusty! We must do something for the dead... for your husband! It isn't correct...

LANDLADY: [*pulling herself together*] No. 'T'ain't decent. [*Picking up* LANDLORD's *pipe, half angrily, half sorrowfully*] 'Is bloody pipe! [*Whimpering, holding the pipe to her cheek*] Coolin' fast... 'Ow I used to hate it... when I'd 'ear the spit cracklin' in the bowl. It was as if Will was doin' it a'purpose. Will did everythink a'purpose...

She gets up.

YOUNG MAN: [*taking* LANDLORD *by the armpits*] See... I'll take like this... [*trying to lift*] and you the feet...

LANDLADY, *blubbering, takes* LANDLORD *by the feet.*

LANDLADY: Ah, Will, Will, who'd ever've thought you wouldn't die in yer bed!

YOUNG MAN: Not too far from it, though. [*Struggling*] Thank the Lord, he... didn't die... in his bath.

LANDLADY: We 'eat the water... Saturdays.

YOUNG MAN: That does... restrict.

They struggle to the bed, deposit the body of LANDLORD—*head at the foot, feet on the pillow.*

LANDLADY: Look, boy, wot we've been an' done!

YOUNG MAN: I'm not surprised. I've never handled such a dead weight. I mean... I...

He begins to hiccup uncontrollably.

LANDLADY: [*as they manoeuvre the body right way around on the bed*] Will was always solid. Even as a young boy... in a photo... Will was a... big... boy...

She tails off into a whimper, which is punctuated by a hiccup from YOUNG MAN.

YOUNG MAN: I'm sorry. Things are somehow never quite... [*hiccup*] ... as they ought to be.

LANDLADY: Don't know about that. [*She bustles to the dresser and takes a cup.*] This nearly always works. [*She fills the cup at the invisible sink.*] I 'ad it from a lady called Mrs Moylan, 'oo was often took this way. [*Handing him the cup*] 'Ere. 'Old yer breath, stick yer fingers in yer ears, count twenty, and drink from the back-side. Then if you're... not better... [*suppressing a whimper*] ... I don't know wot to suggest...

YOUNG MAN: [*trying to carry out some of the acrobatics* LANDLADY *has prescribed, but without giving these exercises his undivided attention*] How did he die, Mrs Lusty?

LANDLADY: 'E just died. Without a word. Without even a fit. [*Holding her face*] Oh, God! Oh, dear!

YOUNG MAN: [*sitting down, holding the cup, thoughtfully*] When it happens, it's easy as that.

LANDLADY: But without even a word! I didn't say goodbye to 'im!

YOUNG MAN: The truth stops where words begin. You would have trotted out the tired sentiments of others. It's better to cry when it's all done... [*Setting the cup on the table*] Or even hiccup... if it takes you that way.

LANDLADY: I could'uv said...

YOUNG MAN: Not you, Mrs Lusty. Don't become obsessed by words.

LANDLADY: You educated people are a jealous lot.

YOUNG MAN: Now and then we do know best.

LANDLADY: I would'uv said... [*She leaves off in a whimper, then slops towards the dressing table at the 'fourth wall'.*] Only Tuesday I said I'd mend 'is jacket. [*Calming*] I went to the theayter instead.

[*Staring out at the audience, into the invisible glass*] They was doin' a drama. [*She begins to take down her hair.*] You wouldn't believe the things that 'appened. They blew up a real bloomin' train! Everybody killed. [*Staring at herself, and other things*] But they all got up at the end, and bowed. There wasn't no... funeral.

She takes up an invisible brush from the dressing table, and begins to brush her hair.

YOUNG MAN: [*nervously, glancing at the dead* LANDLORD] We must do something, Mrs Lusty.

LANDLADY: Wot, again? We only just laid 'im on the bed.

YOUNG MAN: There's always something to be done... before the corpse takes over.

LANDLADY: [*brushing her hair, frantically*] Oh, leave off, can't yer? Leave me to brush me hair! I wish I was at the theayter. There's nothing so snug as red plush... even when you're only lookin' down at it from the gods.

YOUNG MAN: But there's got to be a funeral...

LANDLADY: Don't I know it! That's why Will Lusty died. 'E 'ad it worked out.

YOUNG MAN: But funerals, Mrs Lusty, are nice. Baked meats, and a good, warm cry.

LANDLADY: Oh, I shan't let 'im down. [*Brushing calmly now, but with purpose*] It'll be respectable. It'll be somethink ter talk about. It'll be a 'am funeral.

YOUNG MAN: Am?

LANDLADY: 'Am, silly! Wot you eat. It never was seen in this street. Bill Piper got faggots. And Mrs Ruddock a leg of mutton. But it'll be 'am for Will Lusty, if 'is widow busts!

YOUNG MAN: [*recollecting, to himself*] The first time I'd ever looked at a dead face... And it looked back... as though...

LANDLADY: [*brushing, softly*] Besides, I loved Will. As much as you're allowed to love...

YOUNG MAN: [*to himself*] ... as though he'd intended to do a bunk... to leave me holding the stage... It depends on me in a way it's never done before...

LANDLADY: [*sighing*] If you was allowed to love. But you aren't. And it curdles. It turns sour...

YOUNG MAN: [*appalled*] It depends on me! [*In revolt*] Me! [*Jumping up, shouting at* LANDLADY] For God's sake, stop brushing your hair!

LANDLADY *stands arrested in the act of brushing.*

LANDLADY: [*also shouting*] I must do somethink, mustn't I?

She breaks into a stormy crying.

YOUNG MAN: [*holding his head, speaking rapidly*] Yes, yes, I know! This is the first time anything has happened to me. It's difficult to think.

LANDLADY *goes back to the bed where the body of* LANDLORD *is lying. She slips down beside the bed, huddling, with her head against the side.*

LANDLADY: It's been 'appenin' ter me all me life. From the moment I was born. An' death's the least! [*Taking* LANDLORD'*s hand*] Ah, Will, Will!

YOUNG MAN: [*wincing*] Let us fondle our dead selves! We can't stroke too much… enjoy our sorrow.

LANDLADY: [*rubbing her cheek against* LANDLORD'*s hand*] Why not, I ask? While it lasts. They box it up quick enough.

YOUNG MAN: But other people must have their say. Tell me, Mrs Lusty, are there any relatives?

LANDLADY: [*disgusted*] At least twenty-six.

YOUNG MAN: They must be brought, of course.

LANDLADY: [*dully*] Why?

YOUNG MAN: Why? Because… [*as a bright afterthought*] … why, to eat the ham.

LANDLADY: Ah, the 'am.

YOUNG MAN: And to say the neat, consoling things people do say on such occasions.

LANDLADY: I'll know enough, my lad. I'll know the questions an' the answers.

YOUNG MAN: That's beside the point. It's not what we know. The voices of relatives must express approval. That'll make an honest woman of you.

LANDLADY: [*ruefully*] I'd 'uv thought, by this, that was beside the point, too.

YOUNG MAN: [*imperiously*] Leave it to me, Mrs Lusty. Where do all these people live?

LANDLADY: Number eleven, Ethel Grove.

YOUNG MAN: [*going towards the door, back*] A grey house...

LANDLADY: [*raucously*] ... with the scabs peelin' off...

YOUNG MAN: ... and scurf falling...

LANDLADY: [*infected by a hysterical kind of gaiety*] ... with the windows sealed down...

YOUNG MAN: [*from the door, calling back, triumphantly*] ... because when they're open, the curtains have a habit of waving in the wind!

LANDLADY: [*leaning against the bed, laughing in spite of herself*] I always said you was off yer nut!

YOUNG MAN: Well, so long, Mrs Lusty. I'll be on my way!

He turns and runs up the stairs, two at a time. The stairs and hall light up to receive him.

LANDLADY: [*calling after him*] Cracked!

The basement fades.

YOUNG MAN: [*running upstairs*] I would be... if I stayed... five minutes longer... in this deadly house... I must breathe! [*He pauses for moment in the hall, near the street door. Turning and looking back*] Listen to it! The landlord's called in the last cockroach!

As he exits into the street, a drop falls, concealing the rooms of the lodging house.

SCENE SEVEN

A street.

To be played in front of the drop. Lamp post, right, and a length of kerb-stone to accommodate one character as a seat. Another lamp post, left, under it an overflowing garbage bin.

A LADY *is rummaging through the bin. A* SECOND LADY *is seated, right, on the kerb.*

FIRST LADY, *rather ancient, is dressed in all kinds of splendour: net, lace, all a rusty-black—sequins, a tiara from which the glitter has gone.*

SECOND LADY, *rather more ancient, similarly dressed, but obviously fonder of feathers. A little supper hat, with one sad peacock feather, crowns the whole.*

FIRST LADY: [*rummaging in the bin*] Some people throw away only what they don't need. That's something I noticed soon as I come into the discard trade.

SECOND LADY: But there's always the surprises, dear.

FIRST LADY: Of course. There's the surprises. It's the surprises that keeps yer goin'. [*Out of the bin she fishes a bloater with some of the flesh still on it.*] There! Yer see? There's as pretty a backbone as a person would ever find.

SECOND LADY: To them that cares for fish.

FIRST LADY: [*grande dame*] I can't tempt you, then?

SECOND LADY: Oh, dear, no. It's kind. But I just 'ad a bite… on a corner in Charlotte Street.

FIRST LADY *proceeds to pick the bloater.*

FIRST LADY: [*nostrils suddenly distended over the fish*] That reminds me of something.

SECOND LADY: What, then? You know I try to be well-informed.

FIRST LADY: A bath 'eater.

SECOND LADY: Why a bath 'eater?

FIRST LADY: Why, it blew up, and 'it me in the nose.

SECOND LADY: If you must fiddle with a bath 'eater, of course it'll blow up.

FIRST LADY: Seriously, though, Mrs Fauburgus, it does the pores good to unstop them once in a while.

SECOND LADY: My pores would put up with no such monkey business, Mrs Goosgog. Not on yer life.

FIRST LADY *rummages again in the bin.*

FIRST LADY: Ah, well, it takes all kinds to make a tasty dustbin. [*She draws out a string of enormous pearls. Displaying the necklace*] Do you believe in that one?

SECOND LADY: I've not believed in anythink in life since a copper pinched me maidenhead.

FIRST LADY: [*trying a pearl with her teeth*] Celluloid!

She swallows the pearl.

SECOND LADY: I'm not surprised. There's no tellin' nowadays what won't turn up in celluloid.

FIRST LADY: [*consuming pearls, one by one*] But it has its uses... and is light... and cheap... only a bit monotonous.

She drops the string with the remaining pearls back into the bin.

SECOND LADY: Are there no letters? There's nothink I like better than a read of a good letter. Look and see, Mrs Goosgog, if you can't find us a letter. I'm inclined to feel melancholy at this hour of night.

FIRST LADY: Anything to oblige a friend. But banana skins, Mrs Fauburgus, are fatal to letters.

SECOND LADY: Letters are fatal.

FIRST LADY: [*fishing one out of the bin*] Here's one. It's all mauve.

SECOND LADY: And scenty? It must be scenty.

FIRST LADY: It's scenty alright!

SECOND LADY: [*impatient*] Go on, then, read it!

FIRST LADY: [*reading carefully*] 'Dear Harry... thank you for yours with ex... planations... but I have reached the point where... suf... fering is too ex-cruci-atin'...' [*To* SECOND LADY] Style, eh? [*Continuing*] 'I used to think it was a luxury. I could have suffered and... [*squinting at the letter*] ... suffered. Well, of course, I have... wrote you all this before...'

She squints again.

SECOND LADY: [*anxiously*] Go on, dear. What are yer waitin' for?

FIRST LADY: This letter seems to of got mixed up with the termarter sauce.

SECOND LADY: Oh, dear! That does 'appen to letters.

FIRST LADY: [*deciphering with difficulty*] '... wrote you all this before, and shall continue to write... because it has become a habit... if I do not kill myself...'

SECOND LADY: They do, you know. They go out to the postbox. Then they come in and kill theirselves... just out of devilment.

FIRST LADY: [*meditatively, eating the letter*] What gets inter people? Now, when I was in the circus...

SECOND LADY *comes across to the bin, to rummage.*

SECOND LADY: What was you doin' in the circus, dear?

FIRST LADY: 'Andin' up the swords to my old man.

SECOND LADY: What became of yer old man?

FIRST LADY: 'E swallowed too 'ard.

They look at each other, and scream with laughter.

SECOND LADY: [*rummaging in the bin*] Oh, dear, this ain't a very rich bin.

FIRST LADY: There's no tellin'. The best bits are inclined to work towards the bottom.

> *Enter* YOUNG MAN, *right. He is preoccupied, his coat collar turned up as a protection against night, cold, and thoughts.*

YOUNG MAN: [*hesitating, to himself*] A grey house, where heads will emerge from the windows... scenting a corpse... [*He holds back, right, head down, as if wrestling with his doubts and fears. To himself*] But they'll carry the load. I shall retire again, into a corner, and dream... consider the acts of mercy I never perform, while the box is carried out by the relatives in black. [*He faces the audience with his thoughts.*] It'll be safer then. When I ran out on this charitable errand, leaving the fat, huddled woman, it was because I was afraid. I was afraid of the dead landlord lying on the bed. Once this evening he glimmered for a moment, and I almost saw his soul. But when I looked again, he was dead. That was the landlord! Even alive, he was waiting to putrefy... a mound of uncommunicative flesh. [*Shaking off the vision with loathing*] It'll be safer when he's disposed of. So I run to fetch the relatives.

> *Under the lamp post, left, the two* LADIES *look towards* YOUNG MAN, *longing to sympathise.*

FIRST LADY: [*sighing*] A fair young man, with a fair moustache just beginning! Touch the fluff, and it flies away...

SECOND LADY: A fair moustache once made me cry... when I was young...

YOUNG MAN: [*still to himself, doubting*] So I'll run to fetch the relatives...

FIRST LADY: Daisies and buttercups... what wouldn't I give for a field of grass...

SECOND LADY: ... where hares bed, in nests of grass...

YOUNG MAN: [*to himself*] ... though who knows, perhaps it's safer to cut and run...

FIRST LADY: [*to* YOUNG MAN] Hey... Eustace! Got something on yer mind?

YOUNG MAN: [*putting his hands in his pockets, standing his ground*] Nothing particular, thanks. Who are you?

FIRST LADY: We're two professional ladies.

YOUNG MAN: At your age?

SECOND LADY: [*cackling*] Nao, nao! We're in the bits-and-pieces business.

YOUNG MAN: [*with distaste*] So it seems.

SECOND LADY: Lardy da! At least it 'olds a body together, and that's more than thinkin' never did for no-one.

YOUNG MAN: [*wryly*] Perhaps you've hit the nail on the head.

FIRST LADY: [*skipping forward*] I'll let you into a secret. [*Behind her hand*] We're the knockabout girls of the piece.

YOUNG MAN: I thought it was all knockabout.

FIRST LADY: Yes. But our part won't kill yer.

SECOND LADY: No knives in our garters.

FIRST LADY: Won't tickle yer ribs with anything sharper than a fevver.

YOUNG MAN: I could cry... if it was the Anglo-Saxon thing to do.

SECOND LADY: Go on, dear. Cry. Everythink's meant to come out, whether it's wind or water.

YOUNG MAN: You don't realise. My landlord died.

FIRST LADY: Everyone has a dead landlord... tucked away... somewhere.

SECOND LADY: An' rats galore... eatin' their 'eads orf... after midnight.

FIRST LADY: And paper roses...

SECOND LADY: ... with desperate breff...

FIRST LADY: ... and a mother's love...

SECOND LADY: ... to bail you out.

YOUNG MAN: [*bowing*] Thank you for your sympathy. Lull me some more. Not with love, though.

SECOND LADY: [*running to the bin*] With a bloater?

She whisks the fish skeleton under YOUNG MAN's *nose.*

YOUNG MAN: Cripes!

FIRST LADY: [*running to the bin*] Or tomcat perished Saturday night, tryin' to sneak across Holborn?

About to draw out the cat, she stops. Stares into the bin. Pauses. Lets out a long, thin, terrible scream.

SECOND LADY: [*holding her ears*] Oh, 'ark a'er! She's remembered somethink she lost.

FIRST LADY: Murder! Murder! Murder!

SECOND LADY: It's the bloater. There was never nothink like a bloater for makin' a person repeat. [*She goes and looks into the bin. She too lets out a scream, or a series of dry, gasping retches. Protesting*] 'Ere, it wasn't me!

FIRST LADY: Tell that to the magistrate.

SECOND LADY: It's never so much the perlice…

FIRST LADY: Perlice is easy as cheese. Nao… it's the conscience!

SECOND LADY: [*queasily*] Luvva duck…

> The two LADIES *steal away, supporting each other.*

> YOUNG MAN *has stood transfixed, watching the proceeding. Now he goes slowly but deliberately to look.*

YOUNG MAN: [*staring into the bin, pausing, then very gently*] Poor little fellow! [*Suddenly in revolt, shouting*] There was never such brutality… [*On second thought*] Or was it… so very brutal? [*Again gently compassionate*] You died too soon… or weren't even born. No angel struck you on the mouth, to silence what you already knew. Your love returned into love, without ever feeling the thumbscrew and the rack. Tender, humorous foetus! Such a one the landlady might have carried, and dropped almost without knowing, and tried bitterly to remember. Dreams wear no faces when it is important to identify them. [*Suddenly coming down, forward, protesting*] So much for visions! Who'll ever tell where the flesh begins… or ends? The landlord and the dead child are one. But who am I? [*Calmer*] I'm forgetting, though. It's easy for a poet. While the woman sits in the basement, listening to her memories tick, playing with the ends of her hair, I've failed to produce the relatives… [*turning towards the drop, back*] … though this could be their house.

HOUSE: [*in a long, stony echo, the voice of a cold, old man*] Could be… could be…

SCENE EIGHT

Outside a house.

The house has a closed, grey look. There is a door which opens, and solid steps. The windows of the ground, first, and second floors are visible, and will open.

YOUNG MAN: [*contemplating the facade*] Probably never opened since Will Lusty escaped into life. After that it relapsed... into mutton fat and linoleum. [*Brisker*] But here goes. I've started to tell myself I'm a man of action. [*He mounts the steps, and knocks loudly on the door. Holding his ear to the door, calling*] Anyone there?

A pause.

HOUSE: [*echoing coldly*] Anyone... airrr...?

YOUNG MAN: [*listening*] Someone at a great distance getting into his slippers... and coming... and coming...

HOUSE: [*echoing*] ... com... inggg...

YOUNG MAN *starts back down the steps, holding an arm to his face for protection, as four* RELATIVES *pull up the windows and pop their heads out, one at the ground floor, two at the second, and one at the third. (Alternatively, one could be made to stick his head out of a trap, as if from the basement.) All four* RELATIVES *exactly alike—soap-coloured, lean, with drooping, straw moustaches.*

RELATIVES: [*in unison*] Is it Will?

YOUNG MAN: [*retreating in panic against the lamp post*] Yes!

FIRST RELATIVE: We knew'd it'd be about Will.

SECOND RELATIVE: There was every indication.

THIRD RELATIVE: A knockin' at the door Friday night.

FOURTH RELATIVE: A mouse sang behind the wainscot.

FIRST RELATIVE: So what could you expect?

YOUNG MAN: I don't know, I'm sure. Frankly, though, I expected you to be more rational.

FIRST RELATIVE: What did Will tell yer?

YOUNG MAN: Nothing.

SECOND RELATIVE: Will never spoke.

YOUNG MAN: Only once. And I didn't understand. Then, when I went back to ask, he was already dead.

THIRD RELATIVE: We knew'd it'ud happen. It was a bad business.

YOUNG MAN: You're not suggesting...?

FIRST RELATIVE: [*convinced*] Will Lusty died of his wife.

FOURTH RELATIVE *lets out a thin, lascivious laugh.*

YOUNG MAN: Not really. She even loved him at times… which is the most we can expect of anybody.

RELATIVES *shake their heads.*

THIRD RELATIVE: Never trusted Alma.

FOURTH RELATIVE: Alma Jagg. Of Edmonton.

FIRST RELATIVE: A red, plump girl. She stood on the doorstep, and her arms mottled in the wind.

SECOND RELATIVE: She smelled of milk. And celery.

THIRD RELATIVE: And crushed nettles.

FOURTH RELATIVE *lets out his thin laugh.*

FIRST RELATIVE: She turned into a shrew that no blouse could contain.

YOUNG MAN: That may be. But Will Lusty's dead. And now she's trailing on the floor, like any poor rag. The wind's quite gone out of her.

FIRST RELATIVE: No doubt she wants us to assist in choosin' a decent casket.

YOUNG MAN: That's more or less the idea.

SECOND RELATIVE: And a solid marble stone… with hands clasped in eternal agreement.

YOUNG MAN: We hadn't ventured as far as that. But she'd like you to come. And to the funeral. It will be a…

FIRST RELATIVE: [*nodding his head, ponderously*] … a ham funeral.

YOUNG MAN *starts.*

YOUNG MAN: [*looking at* FIRST RELATIVE] There can't be much that's unexpected.

FIRST RELATIVE: [*sharply*] There's one thing, young man.

THIRD RELATIVE: Very definitely.

YOUNG MAN: Yes?

FOURTH RELATIVE: [*laughing thinly*] What we'd like to know is: Where do you come in?

YOUNG MAN: [*retreating*] I?

FIRST RELATIVE: Yes! You!

YOUNG MAN: [*rattled*] Really, I… I have to find out. You must give me time. Please! There are moments when I can touch fire, but… just now… if you'll accept me as the Greek messenger, I'll be most grateful.

He looks behind him desperately, as if in search of help.

FIRST RELATIVE: [*darkly*] Your shadow's on the ground behind yer.

FOURTH RELATIVE: He still hasn't answered the question.

YOUNG MAN: [*considering*] I haven't, because... people living together
in a house walk with their hands outstretched. Sometimes they
touch one another. But only learn their shapes. That puffy object,
the landlord, should have been obvious enough. He wasn't. He
remained as obscure as the chair on which he sat... complete, but
telling no secrets. At times I hated him for his ugliness and squalor.
I feared his strength. Once, very briefly, I almost loved him. [*Losing
his temper*] Damn you, can't you see I'm obsessed by the landlord?
[*Recovering control, quietly*] Now, will you come? I'll take you to
his dead body.

FIRST RELATIVE: Not so badly put, young man.

FOURTH RELATIVE: [*still suspicious*] Even varnished oak has splinters.

YOUNG MAN: [*at the end of his patience*] I am waiting.

FIRST RELATIVE: I wouldn't be surprised if you didn't 'ave ideas about
yerself. But.... [*with a last look of disapproval*] ... wait till we fetch
our 'at and galoshes.

    RELATIVES *withdraw their heads simultaneously.*

YOUNG MAN: [*coming forward, addressing the audience*] While the
relatives pick their hats from the antlers where they sprout, and
rummage after perished rubber, the dead man has quietly removed
himself. So the funeral will be for the living. That is the funny, or
the tragic part. But we'll eat the landlady's great ham. [*Looking
skyward*] And there'll always be the stars... if they don't begin to
explode in one's face...

    The door of the house opens, and FIRST RELATIVE *appears,
carrying a black bowler hat and loosely-furled umbrella.*

FIRST RELATIVE: [*cheerfully*] There we are!

    He closes the door behind him.

YOUNG MAN: Where are the others?

FIRST RELATIVE: What others?

    FIRST RELATIVE *puts on his hat.*

YOUNG MAN: [*helplessly*] Just as you like. Let's get going then.

    YOUNG MAN *starts to move off smartly.*

FIRST RELATIVE: [*catching him by the arm, restraining him*] Easy does it! I fell down last year at Ramsgate. [*Chuckling*] And Will Lusty can't give us the slip!

    They move off, left.

END OF ACT ONE

ACT TWO

SCENE ONE

The basement.

Same as before, except that the landlord is no longer present, the bed is made, and covered with a quilt, and there is a general swept-and-garnished look. On the kitchen table there is a large boiled ham, bottles, and glasses filled with stout. The four RELATIVES *are dotted about the room, upright on kitchen chairs. On the bed, their four bowler hats. The* LANDLADY *is seated behind the table, monumental in black. Beside her is an empty chair, and on the table in front of it, a full glass. After the curtain rises, the actors hold the picture for a brief space.*

FIRST RELATIVE: [*sighing*] Ah, well!

LANDLADY: [*rousing herself, to* FIRST RELATIVE] Another slice, cousin?

FIRST RELATIVE: I don't mind, Alma. I don't mind…

SECOND RELATIVE: [*to* THIRD RELATIVE] 'E'll mind in the night. There's many a resurrection after 'am.

> *As other thoughts take possession of her,* LANDLADY *momentarily closes her eyes, holds her handkerchief to her mouth.* FOURTH RELATIVE *titters.*

THIRD RELATIVE: Ssh! We must respect the feelin's of the widow.

FOURTH RELATIVE: Still in the mothball stage too.

> LANDLADY *continues to serve the ham, passing a helping to* FIRST RELATIVE.

FIRST RELATIVE: Perhaps on second thoughts, Alma, in these sad circumstances it would be more appropriate not to… stuff.

LANDLADY: [*passionately*] Eat, damn yers! Fill yer bellies! That's wot it's 'ere for!

FIRST RELATIVE: I was only suggestin', of course. Out of propriety.

> FIRST RELATIVE *starts to eat the ham.*

LANDLADY: There's nothink like food. 'Specially now. If you stuff yer mouths, they can't get inter mischief.

FIRST RELATIVE: It was our intention to pay a tribute to our relative 'oo 'as just passed on.

LANDLADY: [*unconvinced*] Or to 'ave a dig at the livin'!

FIRST RELATIVE: [*rising undeterred, formal, dignified*] It remains our intention, Alma, to do the necessary by Will Lusty. 'E was a silent man, certainly, but not one that you could overlook. [*From a great depth*] 'Deep' is perhaps the word for Will. Never ever opened a book, but could read the grain in a table simply by passin' 'is 'and across it... like as if 'e was blind. In the days when 'e kept the little sweet shop out at Croakers' Pond, 'e never needed to 'ear the bell to know customers were on the step. 'E'd go on out, and there 'e'd be, ready to weigh the aniseed balls and lickerish allsorts...

LANDLADY: [*swaying, eyes closed*] And the 'conversations'... Don't forget the 'conversations'... with the motters printed onter them. You wondered whether there was any truth...

FIRST RELATIVE: [*frowning*] We must ask you, Alma, not to...

LANDLADY: ... any truth in wot the printed motters told yer.

FIRST RELATIVE: The truth is told in time, Alma, and don't lick off as easy as the printed motter on a 'conversation'.

LANDLADY *nods her head.*

LANDLADY: The truth was always stickier.

FIRST RELATIVE: Now where was we...? [*Clearing his throat*] If the lady's goin' to allow... The children... Yes! [*Picking up the thread*] Little children would lower their eyes... knowin' that Will would tell what they 'ad not yet thought of. The boys 'oo 'ad not yet learnt to twist the wing off a live bird. Little girls, 'oo 'ad not yet found their way into the cow-parsley and docks, dawdled sweetly... sucking sherbet out of paper bags. Will knew... Pardon me! If 'e didn't interfere in anything 'e saw must 'appen, it was because 'e believed a human bein' must purge 'imself of 'is own evil... like anythin'... well, anythink else. Will was gentle. That was 'is weakness. When I say 'weak', I don't mean 'e wasn't strong. Took up wrestlin' as a 'obby. Got so good, they give 'im a valuable silver belt.

LANDLADY *nods.*

But Will was gentle. Anyways, till the end. 'Ere in this very 'ouse... which nobody would say 'e was not the pillar of... there was never an inmate 'oo did not listen for the landlord's breathin'. Slow and gentle. Risin' out of the depths of the house. Expandin' the walls as if they 'ad been ribs…

LANDLADY *takes a deep breath.*

But Will married. That was the other side of the medal. There 'e wrestled and was thrown. Even out at Croakers' Pond, she developed the 'abit of countin' the ivy leaves as she waited. The bell on the shop door was music. 'Ere in the upper rooms, she would sit with the whores on nights when they felt too damn drab to face goin' on the beat. Sat an' played at cat's cradle. Stitchin' the string into gates an' mattresses. Will knew, of course. Because Will knew. And the goodness in 'im turned to pus. That's wot I reckon 'appened. Will bust at last infected by 'is missus's life. [*Looking at* LANDLADY] Now 'is missus…

LANDLADY: Thanks! I'm not all that simple. I know my life inside out.

She tosses off what remains of her tumblerful of stout.

SECOND RELATIVE: [*leaning forward*] Do you, though?

THIRD RELATIVE: [*whispering*] I wonder!

LANDLADY *stands up quickly, facing all insinuations.*

FIRST RELATIVE: [*not really trying to convince, as he subsides windily into his chair*] She's not afraid.

LANDLADY: No… why should I be afraid…? I'm not afraid… of nothink. Wot is there to be afraid of, anyways?

SECOND RELATIVE: Not the sound of your own feet… on a stone floor… in a deserted house… at dusk?

THIRD RELATIVE: Not the sudden scream of a chair…?

FOURTH RELATIVE: Not the space you press against in the empty bed…?

LANDLADY *tosses her head.*

LANDLADY: Pffh! If I want me flesh to creep, I have a read of the Sunday paper.

FIRST RELATIVE: Or really search in your mind, Alma Lusty?

LANDLADY: [*rounding on him*] 'Ere, wot is this? Wot'uv I done?

FIRST RELATIVE: Whether you done it or not, it's the thought that counts.

LANDLADY: [*knotting her hands*] Will died natural… if that's wot yer mean. So 'elp me!

SECOND RELATIVE: Will didn't die by the knife…

THIRD RELATIVE: … or by any chemist's bottle…

FOURTH RELATIVE: … but 'e might have done.

FIRST RELATIVE: 'E did. Will Lusty died many a time. Time out of mind.

> LANDLADY *tosses her head.*

LANDLADY: [*twisting her apron, laughing hoarsely*] 'Oo 'asn't done a murder… once or twice… in their imagination?

FOURTH RELATIVE: [*coming very close to her*] But nobody's done it so often… or so well.

SECOND RELATIVE: [*approaching her, softly*] Remember 'ow the blood ran, as you turned the knife in 'is side? Your long black hair was wet…

THIRD RELATIVE: [*approaching her, whispering*] Remember 'ow 'is eyes wondered, after 'e put down the glass? 'E 'ad the puzzled, china eyes of a bull… as it folds its legs… and thumps the earth…

> LANDLADY *goes forward, in great agitation, towards the invisible dressing table with its mirror.*

LANDLADY: Leave me alone, can't yer? Wot 'uv I done?

FOURTH RELATIVE: [*laughing his thin laugh*] Ain't we tellin' yer?

FIRST RELATIVE: When you saw that man roll from his chair, Alma Lusty, an' die for the last time, I wonder you screamed!

> LANDLADY *stares horrified at her own reflection in the invisible glass.*

LANDLADY: I screamed 'cause I was afraid…

FOURTH RELATIVE: [*laughing*] She was actually afraid!

LANDLADY: [*still staring at the mirror*] … to see it 'appen at last. I never thought 'e would lie so still. I never thought my heart would beat that loud. [*In horror, to the mirror*] I was afraid somebody might 'ear it.

SECOND RELATIVE: She was afraid!

LANDLADY: But I screamed, too… [*closing her eyes*] … because I loved 'im…

FOURTH RELATIVE: Tt-tt-tt!

LANDLADY: I was ashamed. Will's face saw more than any mirror. Sometimes 'e looked under the skin.

THIRD RELATIVE: So you wanted 'im dead…

LANDLADY: Yes. You wouldn't understand. Not any of yers. You was born all-of-a-piece.

FIRST RELATIVE: We certainly never done a murder, Alma.

LANDLADY: Nor never loved. Exceptin' yerselves… yer hollow faces in the glass… an' the black cockroach, squintin' down at yez off the shelf.

FIRST RELATIVE: Alright. We never loved.

SECOND RELATIVE: We never loved the butcher…

THIRD RELATIVE: … or the baker…

FOURTH RELATIVE: … or the man that reads the gas meter!

FOURTH RELATIVE *shrieks with laughter.* LANDLADY *subsides, exhausted, into the chair in which she was sitting before.*

FIRST RELATIVE: [*pointing to the empty chair beside* LANDLADY, *and the full glass waiting in front of it*] We never loved Will Lusty that much, that we keep an empty chair and a full glass waitin' for 'im, after 'e's dead!

LANDLADY *looks aghast and sideways at something non-existent.*

LANDLADY: [*realising*] That is for a young man wot lodges 'ere. A respectable young feller. Only where 'e's got to now, I don't just know.

FIRST RELATIVE: O-ho!

SECOND RELATIVE: 'E'll come back.

THIRD RELATIVE: 'E'll come back.

FOURTH RELATIVE: Nobody escapes.

FIRST RELATIVE: [*to* LANDLADY] In the meantime, fill up yer glass. It's empty.

LANDLADY *does so with eager hand.*

LANDLADY: You've said the word, cousin. Me spirits are as low as the floor. An' that ain't right.

She swallows half a tumblerful.

SECOND RELATIVE: 'T'ain't.

THIRD RELATIVE: This is a funeral.

FOURTH RELATIVE: Of poor Will Lusty, 'oo was mild as 'am.

LANDLADY: [*feelingly*] Not always, 'e wasn't!

She helps herself to another slice of ham.

SECOND RELATIVE: 'Am 'as been known to protest.

FIRST RELATIVE: [*to* LANDLADY] Will liked a joke, too.

> LANDLADY *sits and stares ahead.*

Eh? Didn't 'e, Alma?

LANDLADY: [*rousing herself, faintly*] Why… yes. Will liked a good laugh.

FIRST RELATIVE: Used to laugh, didn't 'e, when people fell down?

LANDLADY: [*mechanically*] Yes. 'E did.

FIRST RELATIVE: 'Specially when they fell on their behinds?

LANDLADY: Yes. Will laughed loudest.

FIRST RELATIVE: [*accusingly*] Why?

LANDLADY: I don't know.

FIRST RELATIVE: Because it's funny, ain't it?

LANDLADY: [*the idea taking root*] Yes. It's… funny!

> *She sniggers.*

FIRST RELATIVE: And people are not supposed to lose their balance.

LANDLADY: [*beginning to shake*] But they do!

FIRST RELATIVE: [*slapping the table*] They do!

> LANDLADY *begins to lose control.*

LANDLADY: [*laughing*] And are never the same again… Lusty used to say… Will said: A man only 'as to bounce like a ball to know 'ow much of 'is will is free.

SECOND RELATIVE: Our relative was a philosopher…

THIRD RELATIVE: … as well as a wrestler.

FOURTH RELATIVE: It's much the same thing. Eh, Alma?

LANDLADY: 'Ow do I know? [*Drying her eyes*] I don't know nothink. [*About to lose control again*] 'Ave another slice of 'am? [*She bursts. Howling with laughter*] Aoh, go on! Wot 'uv yer done to me? There's nothink ter laugh about… nothink funny at… all… Me ol' man's just… died…

> *At this the four* RELATIVES *roar too. The basement darkens.*

SCENE TWO

Simultaneously young man's bedroom appears. YOUNG MAN *is discovered standing isolated, centre.*

YOUNG MAN: I haven't gone down yet, because I can't face the mourners. Even at a distance you can hear the creaking of their black thighs, and their thin shoulders, green at the seams. How their moustaches twitch and glisten to deliver twisted truths! They are letting the landlady have it, poor cow. She lashes her tail, and tosses her head, and lows. But she can't throw them off. Her conscience sticks to her. Her confused soul lumbers through the labyrinth, laughing when it should cry, and crying when it should laugh. Such confusion is catching. If it weren't for that I might have gone down.

The other bedroom lightens. The GIRL *is standing in its centre, on the same spot and in the same attitude as* YOUNG MAN.

GIRL: Walls are no protection from thoughts. Sorry if I overheard you.

YOUNG MAN: [*indifferent at present*] I'd forgotten you were there.

GIRL: So much the better.

YOUNG MAN: And now that you are, I doubt if I have the strength for one more attitude.

He goes and sits in the plush armchair, GIRL *following suit in the twin in her own room.*

GIRL: [*laughing*] Splendid! One day you may discover you're standing on your own feet.

YOUNG MAN: I no longer care.

GIRL: For the moment you're disgusted by what you begin to suspect may be life.

YOUNG MAN: [*protesting*] That poor Judy they're bashing in the basement? Never!

He jumps up and goes defiantly to the centre of his room.

GIRL: [*neither agreeing nor disagreeing*] Well…

YOUNG MAN: Once I almost took the world in my hands. It was a lovely ball of coloured glass…

GIRL: But it would have broken.

YOUNG MAN: Once I almost wrote a play, in which the situations were too subtle to express.

GIRL: [*ironical*] But the attitudes were your own, and would have given you endless pleasure.

YOUNG MAN: [*going quickly through the hall, to the door of the second bedroom, menacingly*] I didn't ask for any of this!

GIRL: [*going similarly to the door on her side*] Nobody asked for their own misgivings. Now won't you go on?

YOUNG MAN: No. I've dried up.

GIRL: Like the subtle play. And the world has turned to a ball of mud, that stinks and stinks in your hands.

YOUNG MAN: [*after a moment, sheepishly*] Yes.

GIRL: [*rounding on him, furiously*] And don't you think you're responsible? For some of it, at least?

YOUNG MAN: [*also rounding, defensive and aggressive at the same time*] Then what do you expect me to do?

GIRL: [*resting her head against the door, closing her eyes, as if helpless and exhausted*] My dear simpleton! If it could be spoken!

YOUNG MAN: [*spreading the palm of his hand on the door*] Yes. Yes. Doesn't matter. Lie still. I can almost touch you. I can… feel your… cheek… forming under my hand!

GIRL: [*for a moment allowing herself to succumb*] And if I put my mouth to the door, your lips would fit into the groove…

YOUNG MAN: [*resting his cheek against the door*] … and we should be complete… at last…

> GIRL *opens her eyes suddenly, and starts away from the door. Moves towards the centre of her room.*

GIRL: It's so easy to delude oneself.

YOUNG MAN: [*also drawing away from the door, exasperated*] Let us, for God's sake, delude ourselves in some small way!

> *He crosses the hall, and moves towards the centre of his own room.*

GIRL: [*firmly*] You must go now.

YOUNG MAN: [*discouraged*] Where?

GIRL: You know without my telling.

> *There is a wave of laughter from the basement.* YOUNG MAN *listens with obvious distaste.*

YOUNG MAN: [*to* GIRL] You, too! You're forcing me back to the dead landlord… tying him to me… like a great weight…

> *He puts hands to his throat, as if feeling a dead weight that must pull him under.*

GIRL: [*remorseless*] … reminding you of his reality…

Light returns to the basement, disclosing LANDLADY *and* RELATIVES *in the same grouping as before.*

And these people, performing the great conjuring act, out of their shabby opera hat…

YOUNG MAN: These people are less convincing than the landlord himself.

GIRL: … these people are as real, and as unreal, as your own face in the depths of the glass.

LANDLADY *and* RELATIVES *come to life in a tremendous gust of laughter.*

SCENE THREE

The basement.

During the following brief scene the bedrooms above remain lit, the YOUNG MAN *and* GIRL *holding their positions centre of their respective rooms.*

FIRST RELATIVE: [*slapping his thigh, telling a story*] … and then Will took the crowbar in 'is 'ands…

SECOND RELATIVE: Will 'ad big 'ands. With rivers of blue veins…

THIRD RELATIVE: … and a tattooed flooer de lees…

FOURTH RELATIVE: … an' Je… Jesus Christ in a crown of thorns…

FIRST RELATIVE: [*exasperated*] Will Lusty took the crowbar, didn't I say?

LANDLADY: [*to* SECOND RELATIVE, *blearily*] 'Ave another slice of 'am, cousin. It's nice.

FIRST RELATIVE: [*persevering*] 'E took the crowbar!

He stands to re-enact the scene, and LANDLADY *and other* RELATIVES *lean forward, and fix him with bemused attention.*

'E took it in 'is 'ands. And before yer could say knife, 'e'd twisted it into 'andlebars!

SECOND RELATIVE: [*without begging to differ*] A croaky 'oop!

THIRD RELATIVE: A streak of lightnin'!

LANDLADY: I'm buggered if it was anythink of the sort. It was a true-lovers' knot!

FIRST RELATIVE: [*slapping* LANDLADY *on the thigh*] Alma said it!

FOURTH RELATIVE: [*popping his head over* LANDLADY*'s shoulder, giggling*] Alma would!

   All roar.

SCENE FOUR

During the following scene, the basement remains lit. LANDLADY *and* RELATIVES *hold their positions.*

YOUNG MAN: They'll bate her till she's raw and bleeding.
GIRL: Her dreams have been bloodier.
YOUNG MAN: Are you a specialist in tortures?
GIRL: Am I your other self?
YOUNG MAN: My head's reeling with probabilities.
GIRL: Even so… it's time you went down to the others.
YOUNG MAN: [*an automaton*] Time… I… went… down…
GIRL: Aren't you already going?
YOUNG MAN: Yes… I'm… go…
GIRL: To play your part in the charade.

   YOUNG MAN *pauses at the door of the second bedroom.*

YOUNG MAN: [*addressing the door*] And what about you?
GIRL: Oh, I shall be there. Don't worry. I shall be sitting on your right hand!

   GIRL *and her bedroom fade.*

YOUNG MAN: [*mechanically*] And so I return to the basement… if I've ever really left it.

   As he moves towards the stairs, the young man's room and hall fade.

SCENE FIVE

The basement.

The stairs light as YOUNG MAN *descends hesitantly. At same time, the group of mourners in the basement animates again.*

LANDLADY: [*to* FIRST RELATIVE] Another slice, cousin?
FIRST RELATIVE: I don't mind, Alma. I don't mind.

LANDLADY: [*coyly, stifling a belch*] Reminds me of… me weddin' night!

FOURTH RELATIVE: Oo-er, tell us, Alma!

LANDLADY: We 'ad a 'am.

SECOND RELATIVE: [*singing*] 'They wouldn't believe me!
   They wouldn't believe me!'

LANDLADY: A tre-mend-jous 'am! Well, to cut a story short… [*coyly*] …
   because weddin' nights are short…

   Roars from the RELATIVES.

THIRD RELATIVE: [*slapping his thigh*] I bet Alma's was the shortest!

LANDLADY: I wakes, see? There's a slice of light beneath the blind.
   Mornin', see? I turns to my Will. Me, the blushin' bride! ''Oly
   smoke!' I cries. I pulls back me 'and. No Will beside me in the bed.
   Know wot there was?

RELATIVES: [*leaning forward*] What?

LANDLADY: Will, a course… I finds out later… is makin' a cuppa. But
   beside me in the bed… you'll never guess… the bleedin' 'am!

FIRST RELATIVE: What did I tell yer? Will was always a jokey one!

   All roar. YOUNG MAN *has reached the door of the basement, back.
   The stairs fade out. He looks in at the convulsed* LANDLADY *and*
   RELATIVES. *All turn and stare back at him. There is a silence.*

[*At last*] Bless me if it ain't the young lord!

LANDLADY: [*encouraging, to* YOUNG MAN] Why, Fred! Come an' sit
   alongside of me. [*Patting the chair*] Ain't I been dustin' yer chair
   down… all this time?

   On the table, in front of the chair, the full glass is still waiting.

FOURTH RELATIVE: Oho! Fred, eh?

LANDLADY: [*patting the chair, tittering at* RELATIVES] Yes. Didn't yer
   know?

FIRST RELATIVE: No!

   YOUNG MAN *advances shyly, sits on the edge of the chair.*

LANDLADY: [*encouraging*] Don't be afraid, dear. These is friends.

SECOND RELATIVE: A comparatively young man!

THIRD RELATIVE: Quite a boy!

FOURTH RELATIVE: But well-developed!

   Silence.

LANDLADY: [*to* YOUNG MAN] There! Drink, dear.

> YOUNG MAN *sips stout, but without pleasure.*

[*To* RELATIVES] Fred's shy... [*bridling*] when there's company.

YOUNG MAN: [*diffidently*] I wanted to pay my respects to the widow of the...

LANDLADY: [*fuddled*] That's alright, dear. That's over. Now we've begun again.

SECOND RELATIVE: She's right.

THIRD RELATIVE: By 'rithmatick!

FIRST RELATIVE: [*intoning*] If you give it time, even marble recovers its circulation...

FOURTH RELATIVE: ... the nettle is silent that screeched in the gritty wind...

SECOND RELATIVE: ... the eye is dry...

THIRD RELATIVE: ... dry.

LANDLADY: [*sniggering*] Dry! No doubt... [*drinking*] ... about that. Couldn't get me words out without a little bit of assistance. Death's a dry business. [*Remembering something*] Nothing drier... [*tortured*] ... 'xceptin' love...

YOUNG MAN: Look here, do you have to tell them any more?

LANDLADY: I don't have to tell... only what I... believe. But what do I believe... [*touching her bust, looking at her hands*] ... since they took it away from me?

FIRST RELATIVE: [*taking the cue*] Personally I never believed there was a pair of 'ands inside those gloves... wringin' theirselves as the earth fell on the coffin.

FOURTH RELATIVE: An' what about all that plaster stuff they put under glass for funerals? Was you taken in by that? It could have been... sugar. Same as at a weddin'.

LANDLADY: [*patting* YOUNG MAN] They're right, dear. Everythink begins... over and over again.

> YOUNG MAN *has pushed away his glass, continues to stare from one to another of the mourners.*

Drink up, duckie. You an' me's alive!

YOUNG MAN: [*rising, backing away*] But you smell of moth...

FIRST RELATIVE: That's a compliment to pay a widow and 'er relatives!

All laugh, except LANDLADY, *who is becoming maudlin, and* YOUNG MAN, *who is frozen with disgust.*

LANDLADY: [*tearfully*] Why do I deserve this? Everythink slips through me fingers. I got a chill, too, standin' by Will Lusty's grave.

YOUNG MAN: [*to* RELATIVES] How long do you people usually indulge in the sentiments?

FIRST RELATIVE: [*taking it as a hint, rising, very dignified*] No longer than we're wanted.

Other RELATIVES *follow suit.*

SECOND RELATIVE: I assure you!

THIRD RELATIVE: Sentiments, indeed!

FOURTH RELATIVE: Facts as plain as the parson's nose!

LANDLADY: [*peering around, to* YOUNG MAN] 'Ave you put yer foot in it, love?

YOUNG MAN: [*to* RELATIVES] You've had a good laugh. You've buried the dead. Your heads whirl with recollections and lascivious hopes. [*Pointing*] Now, gentlemen, your hats are on the bed.

RELATIVES *get up to take their hats.*

SECOND RELATIVE: [*taking a hat*] The master mind takes over.

THIRD RELATIVE: [*hat in hand*] 'E's welcome.

FOURTH RELATIVE: [*ditto*] We leave you the empty house, young man.

SECOND, THIRD *and* FOURTH RELATIVES *move back, towards the door.*

YOUNG MAN: [*not so sure of himself, almost putting out his hand to stop them*] That's a pretty liberal bequest. After all…

FIRST RELATIVE: [*taking up his hat from the bed*] Did 'e say a empty house? [*Going towards the door*] Not quite! It's got the landlady in it!

RELATIVES *roar. Group for a moment at the door.*

LANDLADY: [*rousing herself*] Wot's all this? Wot about me?

YOUNG MAN: Nothing. The people are going.

RELATIVES: [*singing, to any drunken tune, all together*]
    'Oo can tell
    If the light'ouse bell
    'S ringin' for the wreck

Of the Hesperus?

We only know
That the undertow
'S strong as hell
Round the rocks...

Cheers and jeers from RELATIVES *as they go out to the stairs.*

LANDLADY: [*holding her temples*] Wasn't it somethink about the moon?
    Didn't they put the moon out, Jack?

YOUNG MAN: If they didn't, they'll have a good try. But I shouldn't worry.

LANDLADY: You sound kind, young man.

She looks at him, surprised. RELATIVES *are mounting the stairs.*

RELATIVES: [*singing drunkenly*] We only know
    That the undertow...

LANDLADY: [*still staring at* YOUNG MAN] Kind!

YOUNG MAN: [*sitting down, sighing*] Not really, Mrs Lusty. I've just done
    something which happened to be expedient. That's the way great
    virtues get thrust on people who don't deserve them.

FOURTH RELATIVE: [*on the stairs, singing*]
    Aaooh... me old oak bucket
    Got a 'ole in it,
    Me poor little bucket
    Went down...

SECOND RELATIVE: [*on the stairs*] I'll bloomin' bust if I don't...

OTHER RELATIVES: Sssh!

LANDLADY: [*to* YOUNG MAN] Whatever you tell me, then. I don't know
    much.

RELATIVES *reach the hall, and prepare to negotiate the front door.*

THIRD RELATIVE: [*to the others*] Hey, wait a mo!

FOURTH RELATIVE: [*leaning over the banisters*] Listen to 'em down
    there! They're at it!

YOUNG MAN: [*to* LANDLADY] You know enough. What you're intended
    to, anyway. More than that might seem less generous.

FIRST RELATIVE: [*aping* LANDLADY, *his hand cupped to his mouth,
    calling down into the stairwell*] Another slice of 'am, young man?
    Another slice of 'am?

RELATIVES *cannot contain their laughter as they exit into the street. The door bangs, the stairs and hall darken.*

SCENE SIX

The basement.

LANDLADY: [*accepting* YOUNG MAN *'s statement*] P'raps you understand. You got edgercation. I only know wot I'm told. An' wot I can 'old in my two hands.

She glances at an area window, from which the last malignant light has faded. In herself a faint glimmer of the devil.

But I can always pull the curtains an' make it snug. [*Doing so*] There now? See?

YOUNG MAN *sits staring in front of him, elbows on the table.*

[*Returning to the table*] You think I'm drunk. I'm not. Only tipsy. An' tipsy's warm!

YOUNG MAN *continues disinclined to speak.*

You're down. [*Touching him*] Wot are yer down about?

YOUNG MAN: I was wondering what I could say to you.

LANDLADY: Will didn't wonder. 'E just sat.

YOUNG MAN *shudders, so that* LANDLADY *removes her hand.*

YOUNG MAN: That's what I'm afraid of. Will sat. [*Speaking as stolidly as landlord, but without burlesquing his voice*] He was content. This house is life. I watch my house fill with light, and darken. These are my days and nights. The house spreads solid over my head.

LANDLADY: [*agitated*] Gawd, yes, that was Will! Pull yer neck out, boy, before you fall!

YOUNG MAN: But Will was wise. This table is love, if you can get to know it…

YOUNG MAN *stares in front of him.*

LANDLADY: [*bitterly*] A fat lot Will knew! 'E sat an' stared, an' belched… when the wind got too sour for his stummick.

YOUNG MAN: [*to himself*] … if you can get to know it.

LANDLADY: [*desperate*] Speak to me, can't yer? Before I lose you, too…

She goes impulsively and seizes YOUNG MAN *by the arm, but he gets up and extricates himself.*

YOUNG MAN: Words are bridges that won't bridge. They break.

LANDLADY: [*passionately*] Let 'em!

A silence in which they stand facing each other.

[*Putting a hand to her face*] Wot's wrong?

As YOUNG MAN *continues to look through her, she goes forward to the invisible mirror, stares into it, touches her face.*

Wot's wrong with me?

YOUNG MAN: I saw your face.

LANDLADY: It's the same one, ain't it?

She turns on him angrily.

YOUNG MAN: I saw your face!

LANDLADY: [*glancing again at the mirror*] 'T'ain't worn all that well… but 't'ain't all that bad. Gentlemen still turn round on cold days. I 'ad a colour once.

YOUNG MAN: I saw your face. It was horrible!

LANDLADY: [*trembling with rage*] Then why the hell 'uv you only just made up yer mind? You've seen it often enough. Get out, you dirty bastard! Get out! I'm tired…

YOUNG MAN *turns to go.*

Pack yer traps, an' let me 'ear the door bang. So's I'll know.

YOUNG MAN *goes towards the door, back.*

[*Putting out her hand*] No, boy. Don't! I'll be alone then. Don't go! I got a face like a stewed rag. I know. But don't go!

YOUNG MAN *turns at the door, though it is not yet clear whether he means to stay or leave.*

[*Eagerly, placing a kitchen chair*] There, boy! Sit!

YOUNG MAN: [*ironically, but sadly*] And you will be less alone…?

He comes back and sits on the chair, mechanically, LANDLADY *standing beside him, like a ventriloquist beside a doll.*

LANDLADY: [*in a washed-out voice*] There! Comfy?

YOUNG MAN: [*sighing, but dutifully*] Yes.

LANDLADY: Let me take your 'and.

YOUNG MAN: [*without really protesting*] Am I a child?

LANDLADY: Less. You'd find out, Jack, if I was to 'old yer 'ead against my breast.

YOUNG MAN: I'm weaned, you know.

LANDLADY: No man ever really leaves the breast. That's our weapon. The softest weapon in the world.

> YOUNG MAN *detaches his hand.*

YOUNG MAN: So well armed. Then why are you afraid of losing?

LANDLADY: Nothing is all that certain. [*Inspired*] I'd wrap you up with me best kid gloves, an' put you in a box, an' lock it tight.

YOUNG MAN: No go! Thieves can break in while you're out at the grocer's.

LANDLADY: This is all talk, Jack. I'll show you!

YOUNG MAN: [*edgy*] How?

> *She gets up, moves away. The following scene is played like a kind of ritual dance.*

LANDLADY: Well… [*twitching the corner of her apron, speaking in a light, bantering tone, that is also determined and tentative*] … I'll give you presents.

> *She follows* YOUNG MAN.

YOUNG MAN: [*moving away*] What?

LANDLADY: Box of pencils.

YOUNG MAN: No-no.

LANDLADY: A toffee apple.

> YOUNG MAN *laughs, shakes his head. Continues moving away, with* LANDLADY *following.*

I'll give you a kiss to remind yer of yer mother.

YOUNG MAN: I'd always hoped I was an orphan.

> *He moves away.*

LANDLADY: A nice, soft doorstep, then!

> *She snatches at him. He avoids. Retreats behind a chair.*

YOUNG MAN: Not if I know it!

LANDLADY: [*quickening her pace*] Oh, dear, you can never lessen the distance! You can never explain to a person!

YOUNG MAN: Why try? When the meaning's panting down his neck…
LANDLADY: It ought to be made… easier.
YOUNG MAN: This isn't… exactly… algebra.
LANDLADY: Algy…? Algy 'oo?
YOUNG MAN: A dry… standoffish kind of… fellow…
LANDLADY: That seems to be the sort… it's my luck… to get in with.

Silence, broken by action and panting, grabbing, stifled laughter and escape.

[*In pursuit, heated*] You lead a woman a fine dance!
YOUNG MAN: Of which she knows every step.
LANDLADY: [*laughing*] Round and round, eh?

He upsets a chair in her path.

YOUNG MAN: And nothing barred.
LANDLADY: [*laughing, breathless, but pursuing*] It's all in the game…
YOUNG MAN: … of deadly earnest…

LANDLADY continues to pursue, still laughing, but silent now, from chair to chair.

… until you have him exhausted.

He flops down on a chair, right.

LANDLADY: Then it's lovely. [*Advancing on him*] That is closest. All tired lads are ready to be touched. [*Holding the back of her hand to his cheek*] Feel?
YOUNG MAN: [*fascinated, but repelled*] You're all feelers. Your thoughts, even, put out tentacles. Memory becomes an octopus.
LANDLADY: I don't know about that. [*Almost in recitative*] But I was never a slow one. Nor cold. A cold colour, but not cold. Alma Jagg breathed life into the hedges. The frost melted when I lay beneath 'awthorns. I touched the warm, moist earth with my 'and. Afterwards, when flowers come, I lay back… an' crushed 'em. [*Closing her eyes*] 'Ow they smelt, Fred! Remember?
YOUNG MAN: [*stirring uneasily, also in recitative*] The green smell of young sap… Yellow pollen on your nose… The crisscross pattern on your cheek, which had suffocated flowers…

He turns and looks up at her, as if dependent on her for the vision he cannot quite accept.

LANDLADY: [*triumphantly, looking down into his eyes*] Well? An' didn't the clouds sail then? When we looked up at them through the trees?

YOUNG MAN: I looked at clouds...

Withdrawing from LANDLADY, *he moves away into a remoter corner of the kitchen.*

[*Shamefaced*] ... only I didn't realise you were looking too.

LANDLADY: [*alone and absent*] Clouds don't sail that way... not now... not that I've seen for some time.

YOUNG MAN: [*recovering self-possession, laughing bitterly*] You're a spellbinder, you are! You know how to ring the changes.

LANDLADY: Wot else 'as a person got? That, an' the theayter.

YOUNG MAN: You played me, alright!

LANDLADY: Aoh, Fred, 'ow you create!

YOUNG MAN: Cut out the Fred. It doesn't fit.

LANDLADY: 'T'ain't a question of names. [*She goes to him again.*] An' you know it isn't, Fred! [*Taking him by the arms, above the elbows*] That's why I can feel yer tremble!

YOUNG MAN: [*to himself*] ... for my own thoughts.

LANDLADY: Do yer know so much?

YOUNG MAN: Or is it for your neck?

He puts his hands on her throat.

LANDLADY: [*scornfully*] Why, you 'ave grown into a man! A man's always ready to kill a woman for 'is own thoughts.

YOUNG MAN: Then, you are afraid?

LANDLADY: Not afraid. [*Backing*] No-one knows wot they're capable of. That's all.

YOUNG MAN: [*flatly, following*] You're afraid. The truth is terrible before you know it. Then... when you do... it becomes most terrible.

LANDLADY: [*backing against the side of the bed*] There are times when you got to try yer luck.

YOUNG MAN *follows. Stretches out his hand like an automaton.*

[*Putting his hand in her breast*] See? I can't 'elp it if I tremble too. Aoh, Fred, I'm in a proper uproar! [*Taking him in her arms*] Let me 'old yer! Put yer 'ead 'ere... close to me neck... where it fits... warm!

YOUNG MAN: And let the senses finish me off!

LANDLADY: You'll soon learn where yer hinges are!

YOUNG MAN: [*half triumph, half disgust*] I'm learning!

> *Difficult to tell whether he is drawn down by* LANDLADY, *or whether he topples her backwards on the bed in their all-absorbing embrace.*

LANDLADY: This way the clock stops…

YOUNG MAN: This way the sea sucks… but under… under…

LANDLADY: [*as her mouth takes possession of his*] Wot price yer bloomin' poetry now?

> YOUNG MAN *begins to struggle against her.*

YOUNG MAN: [*struggling*] I'm damned if I'll wear the landlord's old glove!

LANDLADY: I could die…

YOUNG MAN: [*trying to wrench himself free*] I'm… damned…

LANDLADY: … willin'ly…

> *Brief silence; panting and struggle.*

YOUNG MAN: [*brutally, quickly, between his teeth*] You'll never sink me deeper than I've sunk!

LANDLADY: That's not… I never lived… only now…

YOUNG MAN: So they say!

LANDLADY: True enough. But no-one never ever believes.

> YOUNG MAN *at last succeeds in wrenching himself free. Puts his knee on her stomach, hands on her throat. Presses.*

YOUNG MAN: [*viciously*] Then, die… then. Die…!

LANDLADY: [*strangled scream*] Ahhhhhhhh!

> LANDLADY *tears herself away, staggers, falls forward onto the floor, centre, crying.*

YOUNG MAN: Lie there in your own sweat! I'd call you 'whore' if I hadn't made you one.

LANDLADY: [*gasping and crying*] You didn't kill me, Jack, but couldn't 'uv done a better job if you 'ad.

YOUNG MAN: You'll recover… and enjoy your bruises. You've as good as shown us that already.

LANDLADY: I'm a woman, I suppose.

YOUNG MAN: But flesh, unfortunately, isn't the final answer.

LANDLADY: Get out, then... now that you've seen me.

YOUNG MAN: My legs have never been more willing.

YOUNG MAN *goes out, back. The stairs light.*

LANDLADY: [*in a renewed burst of sobbing*] Oh, God! Will! Will! I don't know wot I done... to be shut up in this body... an' nobody to open it an' let me out...

The basement fades.

SCENE SEVEN

The stairs.

YOUNG MAN: [*running up the stairs, jubilantly*] I could clear this old frayed carpet at one leap... catapult into the night... let the cold clean me... [*Pausing near the top*] Down below, a fat woman lies crying on the flags, a last slobber of passion on her mouth... Ugh! [*He continues to mount, slower.*] Anyhow, she's disposed of. I am free. I couldn't have made a better escape if she'd been packed into a box along with the landlord. [*He pauses on reaching the hall.*] I... am free... aren't I? Or has the prig simply taken over? I am a poet, I said. I shall possess the infinite. Or am I just an ineffectual prig, looking at the world through a telescope... [*hesitating outside his own door*] ... through the wrong end?

His room lights up, but he does not enter. The stairs fade.

SCENE EIGHT

The hall and, subsequently, both bedrooms.

YOUNG MAN *walks quickly across the hall to the door of the second bedroom.*

YOUNG MAN: I must know. You! Tell me! [*He bangs on the closed door.*] Are you there?

The adjoining room remains in darkness.

[*Thumping wildly*] What's happened? Has the door thickened? Have you left me? Hello! Can't you see I'm desperate?

The adjoining room slowly lightens. GIRL *is seated on an upright chair on the farther side, her back to the door. Her expression is severe.*

GIRL: [*coldly*] Everyone is desperate.

YOUNG MAN: Yes… of course… but in a crisis, it's only human to ask for a sign. And I do ask for some sign.

GIRL: [*sadly*] You must look in your own heart.

YOUNG MAN: But I am I.

GIRL: And what am I… but you?

YOUNG MAN: It's true, then…

GIRL: [*gently*] I was ashamed just now.

YOUNG MAN: When?

GIRL: Down there in the basement.

YOUNG MAN: There was no other way out.

GIRL: [*sighing*] No. [*She gets up from her chair.*] Not yet. You weren't up to it. [*She advances towards the separating door.*] The landlady has won the round.

YOUNG MAN: Won?

GIRL: No doubt about it. [*During the following, she moves restlessly about the room.*] She lies in a heap on the kitchen floor. Her only medals are her bruises. Smudgy, sludgy Mrs Lusty! Bust! But she still has her simplicity. That's one bridge the devils fail to destroy in leaving. She doesn't know it yet… listening, snively, to the clocks. Her innocence has even dredged a kind of beauty out of the ruins of her face. If you had stayed, you might have recognised, and forgiven.

YOUNG MAN: [*dismissing the possibility, with disgust*] I held her sweaty body…

GIRL: … in which the life beat and struggled.

YOUNG MAN: Her face was hideous…

GIRL: … hoping she might express herself… just that once more.

YOUNG MAN: [*contemptuously*] Express!

GIRL: Those who live also create.

YOUNG MAN: In that case… I have nothing more to say.

    GIRL *comes close to the door.*

GIRL: [*now tender and persuasive*] No. You are beginning. There is no end where there is beginning. Beginning must follow end. Endlessly.

[*Making of it an incantation*] On many future occasions you'll wrestle with the figures in the basement... passion and compassion locked together. Sleepers are stirring in other rooms to hear their dream interpreted in words. The hands are curled... waiting to open.

YOUNG MAN *leans his head against the door, lulled by possibilities. His face is full of wonder.*

Your eyes see already.

YOUNG MAN: Only yours will convince me. [*Hardening*] I'll smash the door if necessary!

GIRL: [*again severe*] Never!

YOUNG MAN: We'll see!

GIRL: [*a long, cold cry*] Never!

YOUNG MAN *starts to rattle the door handle, then to batter the door itself with his fist, then his shoulder.*

YOUNG MAN: You realise...? You've lost control of your puppet...

As he continues to batter the door, the figure of GIRL *is seen moving desperately about the room, almost like a bird in a cage, in search of a possible avenue of escape.*

GIRL: [*panic-stricken*] Break, then!

YOUNG MAN: [*throwing his weight against the door*] I'll... run the... risk...

GIRL: [*poised, waiting for the decisive moment*] ... and find nothing!

As YOUNG MAN *bursts through the door, staggering, and still off balance,* GIRL *disappears into thin air, i.e. she slips behind the gauze wall, back, as the lights fade from it. Before her exit, she must let fall a spray of white lilac from the folds of her skirt.*

On entering, YOUNG MAN *looks quickly around the deserted room, touches the air.*

YOUNG MAN: [*dazed*] She was right. We never meet... [*putting his hands to his eyes*] ... for more than a moment. Foolish of me to have expected more... [*He stands swaying, looking down. At a loss*] What's this? [*He stoops and picks something up.*] A spray of lilac. White lilac! How we wrote... the pale, exquisite verses of adolescence... to find they have turned... [*crushing the lilac, throwing it away*] ... brittle!

[*He leans against the frame of the communicating door.*] At least the landlady's poem speaks... after the fashion of imperfect flesh. [*He crosses the hall, wearily enters his own room.*] Lunging and plunging, she raped life, and won... [*throwing himself on his bed*] ... whereas my attempts have amounted to little more than acts of self-abuse in an empty room. [*He lies on his back, looking up at the ceiling.*] Well, here we are... back where we began... amongst the everlasting furniture. This bed on which the nights creak... [*Rolling over onto an elbow, indicating*] The washstand's not ambiguous. Or dressing table... except perhaps the reflection in the glass. [*Touching his actual face*] But the bones are there. [*He gets up, goes and looks into the mirror.*] The eyes can see. And all the time, life of a kind has been seeping through the cracks in this house... [*going to window*] ... flowing through the streets in waves of faces. [*He lays his cheek against the pane.*] If I go down myself, I am swallowed up. Or else... [*slowly, thoughtfully leaving the window*] ... or else...

He goes out into the hall.

As YOUNG MAN *finishes his soliloquy, an actual* GIRL *lets herself in at the front door. The wordless part should be played by the same actress who has appeared as the insubstantial anima. The actual* GIRL *is pale, dreary, rather catarrhal, wearing gold-rimmed spectacles, dowdy hat, street coat—clothes all of an indeterminate colour. She goes immediately into the bedroom in which the girl-anima materialised, closes the door, and is occupied with a certain amount of humdrum business before she is faded out—i.e. she can remove her hat and coat, blow her catarrhal nose, chafe hands, run a hand over the dressing table for dust, swallow a couple of aspirin with the help of a glass of water, and so on, provided everything is very prosaic.*

[*Glancing back at* GIRL, *laughing softly, compassionate rather than contemptuous*] Phyllis Pither! [*He approaches the stairs. Calling*] Mrs Lusty! [*Starts to go down. Calling*] Are you fit to be seen? [*He continues to descend. After a pause*] Or are you still a dreadful sight?

YOUNG MAN *reaches the basement door. Hesitates.* GIRL *in the room above is faded out.*

SCENE NINE

The basement.

YOUNG MAN: [*still outside the door*] Are you there, Mrs Lusty? I've come
to say goodbye. I'm going away.

> *The basement lightens. The stairs and hall die.*

> YOUNG MAN *goes into the kitchen, where* LANDLADY *is lying in
> the same position as before.*

What, still there!

> *He goes towards her, purposefully now.* LANDLADY *stirs, and sits
> up, grimacing at her own stiffness, supporting herself on one arm.*

LANDLADY: Did I dream a man called Will Lusty died? And you…

> *She looks at* YOUNG MAN, *and quickly decides to say no more.*

YOUNG MAN: Who's to say where the dream begins… ever… whether it's
a dead landlord, or a declaration of love.

LANDLADY: I expect it 'appened, boy. All of it. It does! Besides, I still
got the bloomin' 'am between me teeth. An' me mouth's all dry from
stout and argy-bargy.

YOUNG MAN: [*holding out his hand*] Come on!

LANDLADY: [*smiling*] It was a lovely funeral, though.

YOUNG MAN: Better get up, or your machinery'll stay cockeyed.

> *He helps her, and she gets to her feet painfully.*

LANDLADY: [*wincing*] Aoh! Me bloody bones 'ave turned to stone!

> *She rubs her cold arms.*

YOUNG MAN: That sounds better!

LANDLADY: If it's language yer mean, I know ladies 'oo get 'igher marks.
[*She goes to the table, and sits down at it.*] Wot's all this about yer
goin' away?

YOUNG MAN: Yes. Tonight. At once.

LANDLADY: Wot's got into yer?

YOUNG MAN: I… don't know.

LANDLADY: An' where are yer goin'?

YOUNG MAN: I don't know that either.

LANDLADY: Wot a lather of nothink! An' yer socks not darned! Did you pack yer things?

YOUNG MAN: You know I haven't any. Except the spare shirt. And I lost that.

LANDLADY: Well, things do happen. And 'ere's me… a relic! [*Nodding*] A relic alright when you're gone! [*Loudly*] You know, I quite like you, yer little bugger!

YOUNG MAN: That's why I came to say goodbye. [*He pauses.*] Well…

LANDLADY *gets up. Goes slowly towards him.*

LANDLADY: Then it's goodbye, Jack.

She takes his hand in both hers, holding it to her.

YOUNG MAN: Goodbye, Mrs Lusty.

He allows her to hold his hand for a moment, then takes her face in his hands, and kisses her on the forehead.

LANDLADY: You 'aven't been that close, Jack… not since I carried yer.

YOUNG MAN: [*quickly*] We'll waste a lot of words if I don't get going.

He turns towards the door. The stairs and hall light up. YOUNG MAN *runs up the stairs.*

LANDLADY: [*following to the basement door, watching, calling after him*] So long, boy! Send us a pitcher postcard now and agen! Let's know you're alive and kickin'! But write plain.

YOUNG MAN *turns at the top of the stairs.*

YOUNG MAN: [*calling back*] So long, Mrs Lusty! I'll be on my way!

LANDLADY: [*at breaking point*] Then go, boy! Go! Go!

The basement and stairs fade. Only the hall remains lit.

SCENE TEN

The hall.

YOUNG MAN *pauses a moment in the hall.*

YOUNG MAN: [*thoughtfully*] How warm her face was… [*going towards the front door*] … and touching… [*opening the door on a night placid with moonlight*] … lovely in its way… the way of those who've lived, and confessed, and survived their own confession.

Well, here's the street. [*Looking out through the doorway*] The night was never stiller, or closer, I could put out my hand and touch it… like a face…

> *He leaves the house, goes into the street. As the door closes the whole of the back wall dissolves, so that* YOUNG MAN *is seen walking into the distance through a luminous night.*

THE END

www.currency.com.au

Visit Currency Press' website now to:

- Buy your books online
- Browse through our full list of titles, from plays to screenplays, books on theatre, film and music, and more
- Choose a play for your school or amateur performance group by cast size and gender
- Obtain information about performance rights
- Find out about theatre productions and other performing arts news across Australia
- For students, read our study guides
- For teachers, access syllabus and other relevant information
- Sign up for our email newsletter

The performing arts publisher

www.ingramcontent.com/pod-product-compliance
Lightning Source LLC
Chambersburg PA
CBHW041933090426
42744CB00017B/2043